Great Northern Walks:
Where to Stay

Great Northern Walks: *Where to Stay*

Compiled
by
John Morrison

Pennine Way
Coast to Coast Walk
Cleveland Way
Dales Way
Settle-Carlisle Way

Great Northern Walks: Where to Stay

Published by Leading Edge Press and Publishing Ltd, The Old Chapel, Burtersett, Hawes, North Yorkshire DL8 3PB
Tel: (0969) 667566

© Leading Edge Press and Publishing Ltd, 1991

This book is copyright under the Berne Convention. All rights are reserved. Apart from any fair dealing for research, private study or review as permitted under the Copyright Act, 1956, no part of this publication may be reproduced, stored in a retrieval system, or transmitted in any form or by any means electronic, mechanical, photocopying, recording or otherwise, without the permission of the copyright holder.

British Library Cataloguing in Publication Data

Morrison, John, 1951-
Great Northern Walks: Where to Stay
1. England. Vacation accommodation.
I. Title
647.94427

ISBN 0-948135-24-7

Photography: John Morrison
Cover & maps: Barbara Drew
Type: Leading Edge Press & Publishing Ltd
Printed and bound by Ebenezer Baylis and Son Ltd, Worcester

CONTENTS

INTRODUCTION

With our increased leisure and greater awareness of environmental issues, it's only natural that we should be drawn to walking in the country. And while many people think of walks in terms of hours rather than days, an increasing number of walkers are tackling long-distance trails.

Since the Pennine Way was pioneered in 1965, a startling number of other long-distance walks have been inaugurated. Some are "official", in that the routes are recognised by the Countryside Commission and local authorities, are waymarked on the ground and appear on maps and are described in books. Other walks are simply the happy inspiration of individual hikers, who link together rights of way through interesting terrain and give the resulting route an appropriate name. Long-distance walks are proliferating at such a rate, in fact, that an organisation — the Long Distance Paths Advisory Service — has been set up specifically to keep track of them.

This book concentrates on five major walks in the North: the Pennine Way, Dales Way, Cleveland Way, Coast to Coast Walk and the Settle-Carlisle Way. All five walks have books devoted to them, which describe the route in detail and give information about what can be seen along the way. Walkers attempting these routes should pack one of the guidebooks in their rucksacks along with the appropriate Ordnance Survey maps.

This book does not attempt to duplicate the information to be found in these guidebooks, a number of which are listed in the appendix. We have concentrated instead on where to stay: a vital aspect of long-distance walking that the guidebooks tend, necessarily, to skip over — perhaps mentioning just a few hostels, bunkbarns and campsites.

It is reassuring, when tackling a long walk, to know that a bed — and perhaps an evening meal — will be available at the end of each day's hike. Looking for bed & breakfast accommodation by knocking on doors is time-consuming and frustrating; worse, there is no guarantee of success. During the summer months, and at weekends throughout the year, many hostels, b & bs and inns will be fully booked. Don't risk having to sleep in a hedge-bottom; let your fingers do the walking instead, by phoning some of the numbers in this book before you don your rucksack.

Walkers tend to set out confidently, expecting to finish their chosen route on time. However, a few days of foul weather, peat bogs and blisters can soon begin to erode their enthusiasm. So think twice before pre-booking for

A solitary rambler near Ingleborough in the Yorkshire Dales, epitomising one of the pleasures of long-distance walking: getting away from it all.

every night of your walk. Your progress may be slower (or even faster) than you had anticipated when you pored over the books and maps in the comfort of your sitting room.

A more practical option — unless you can make a very realistic assessment of your speed and stamina — is to pre-book accommodation only for the first few nights. Take this book with you, and phone ahead as you go. Allow, too, for rest days — to put your aching feet up or take in the sights. The limestone area around Malham Cove and Gordale Scar, for example, is well worth taking a day out to explore.

We have taken great care to ensure that all the entries in this book are correct and up-to-date, but we accept no responsibility for any errors or changes that have occurred since going to press. Prices may fluctuate; businesses may change hands and even close down altogether. It must be remembered, too, that many establishments (and particularly campsites) will be closed "out of season".

The information in this book should therefore be regarded as a guide; write or phone for full details about the facilities that each type of accommodation can offer, and whether there are vacancies on the nights you want. You will be courting disappointment if you turn up unannounced, expecting a bed for the night.

For your convenience we have given the full postal address for each entry. Check the exact location of your intended overnight stop. Many farmhouses and bunkbarns, for example, are some distance from the towns whose postal addresses they bear. When in doubt, ask for a map reference. You may also wish to check whether evening meals — and perhaps packed luches — are available.

Accomodation is listed under the following categories: Hotels/Inns, Guesthouses/B & Bs and Budget — which comprises youth hostels, bunkbarns and campsites. Some establishments listed offer more than one type of accommodation (such as camping and bed & breakfast).

Some establishments have paid to have their entries extended or printed in a bold type; walkers can be particularly sure of a warm welcome here.

The guide prices listed are for overnight accommodation for one person, plus breakfast, except for those in the budget section (youth hostels, bunkbarns and campsites) which are for overnight stay only. Prices given for Youth Hostels are for members over 21, and do not include food. Overnight accommodation is cheaper for junior members.

Most youth hostels provide evening meals, as well as kitchens for hostellers who prefer to cook their own food. To stay at a hostel you must be a member of the Youth Hostels Association. You can enroll by post (address in Appendix) or on arrival at any hostel.

When staying at a hostel you must use a sheet sleeping bag. You can buy these at outdoor shops, or you can hire one, for a small charge, when you arrive at a hostel.

The five routes in this book are well provided with hostels. Pennine Way walkers, for example, can stay at hostels for most nights during their walk.

Camping barns and bunkbarns tend to be more basic. Some are little more than "stone tents", with wooden sleeping platforms, unisex accommodation and no cooking facilities, Others offer well-appointed kitchens and a greater level of comfort.

Many walkers will be glad of a few more creature comforts at the end of each day, so we have included a wide range of other accommodation — from cosy guesthouses to country inns and small hotels.

The publishers are keen to ensure that future editions of this book will be as accurate and as comprehensive as possible. So we welcome your comments, amendments and recommendations of any establishments we may have inadvertently missed out.

Happy walking!

PENNINE WAY

The Pennine Way is the "grandaddy" of long-distance walks in this country: the first one to be officially designated as such, in 1965. It was Tom Stephenson, a tireless campaigner for public access to the countryside, who proposed this 250-mile route along the backbone of England.

It is usual to walk the Pennine Way from south to north, so most people begin from the village of Edale in the Peak National Park. The route follows the high ground of the Pennine hills, passing through three national parks and all the northern counties — though hikers spend more that half of the walk in Yorkshire. The end of the trail is the village of Kirk Yetholm, just over

A walker enjoying a section of the Pennine Way that winds through the South Pennine hills.

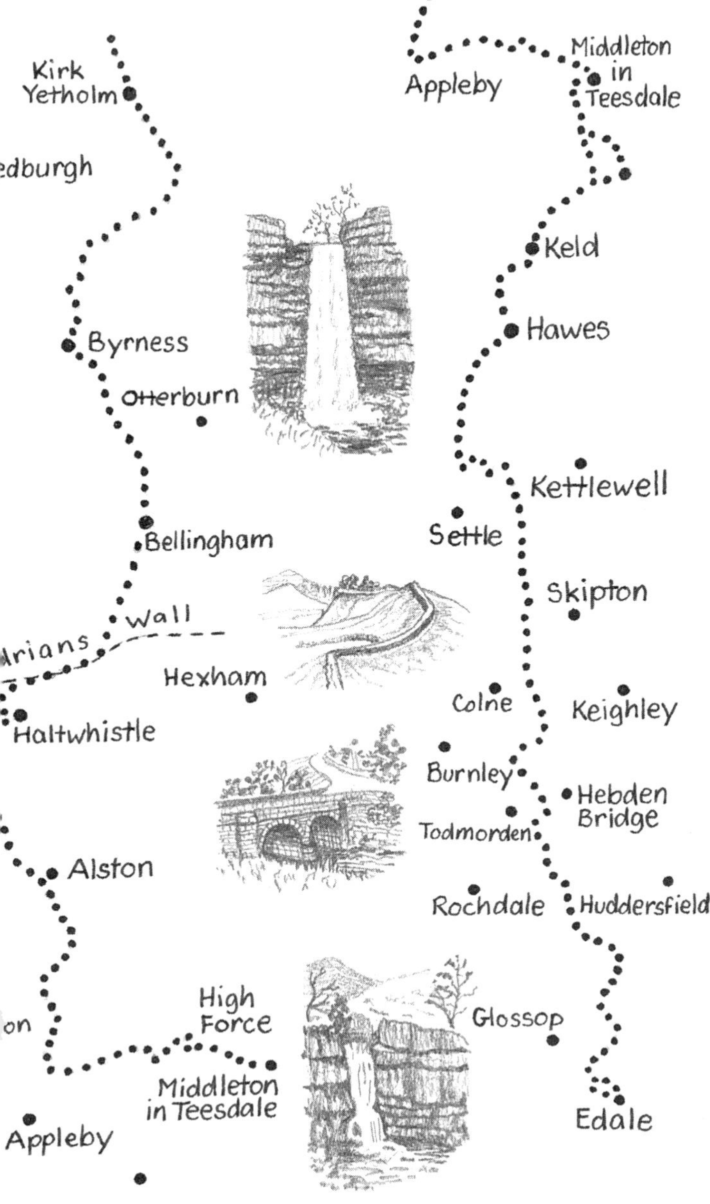
Kirk Yetholm
edburgh
Byrness
Otterburn
Bellingham
Wall
drians
Hexham
Haltwhistle
Alston
on
High Force
Middleton in Teesdale
Appleby
Appleby
Middleton in Teesdale
Keld
Hawes
Kettlewell
Settle
Skipton
Colne
Keighley
Burnley
Hebden Bridge
Todmorden
Rochdale
Huddersfield
Glossop
Edale

the border in Scotland.

While basically an upland walk, the Pennine Way offers a variety of scenery, from Pennine heights to riverside rambles. A number of interesting features are passed on the way: the waterfalls of Hardraw Force (the highest "single drop" in England) and High Force, the moors made famous by the writings of the Brontë sisters and the spectacular limestone scenery of Malham Cove and Gordale Scar.

The walk visits Hadrian's Wall, splendid old castles, squat churches of the Yorkshire Dales, the industrial heartland of Calderdale and stone-built houses of Pennine villages — clustered together to withstand the extremes of northern weather.

The Pennine Way remains a major challenge; if you make it all the way to Kirk Yetholm you can feel justifiably proud of yourself. Fit walkers should allow three weeks to complete the route; unfit walkers shouldn't attempt it at all!

There is no reason, of course, why walkers should attempt the Pennine Way in a single stretch. Those who do, however, will need to think carefully about overnight accommodation. Whether you allocate two weeks, three weeks, or just three days (yes, the Pennine Way *has* been run in that time...), you should ensure you have a bed booked for the night. Having spent all day negotiating a peat bog, you certainly won't relish the idea of hunting for a hostel or guesthouse.

The Youth Hostels Association runs the Pennine Way Bureau for its members. Pennine Way walkers can, with a single letter, pre-book nights at any of the 18 hostels along the route (details in the Appendix). And if you're not a member, then it's about time you were...

There is no specific schedule for covering those 250 miles; it is up to walkers to estimate how far they wish to walk each day. But here is a suggested timetable, with approximate daily mileage:

Edale to Crowden (15)
Crowden to Hebden Bridge (22)
Hebden Bridge to Lothersdale (17)
Lothersdale to Malham (16)
Malham to Horton-in-Ribblesdale (15)
Horton-in-Ribblesdale to Hawes (13)
Hawes to Keld (12)
Keld to Bowes (12)
Bowes to Langdon Beck (19)
Langdon Beck to Dufton (15)
Dufton to Alston (18)
Alston to Once Brewed (22)
Once Brewed to Bellingham (16)
Bellingham to Byrness (15)
Byrness to Kirk Yetholm (27)

EDALE

Hotels/Inns

Rambler Inn,
Edale,
Near Sheffield,
Derbyshire S30 2ZA
Tel: (0433) 70268
Guide Price: £15-17.50

Stonecroft Hotel,
Edale,
Near Sheffield,
Derbyshire S30 2ZA
Tel: (0433) 670262
Guide Price: from £15

Guesthouses/B & Bs

Mrs Chapman,
Brookfields,
Barber Booth,
Edale,
Near Sheffield,
Derbyshire S30 2ZL.
Tel: (0433) 70227
Guide Price: £11

Mrs Beney,
The Old Parsonage,
Grindsbrook,
Edale,
Near Sheffield,
Derbyshire S30 2ZD
Tel: (0433) 70232
Guide Price: £9.50

Budget

Hostel (YHA),
Rowland Cote,
Nether Booth,
Edale,
Near Sheffield,
Derbyshire S30 2ZH
Tel: (0433) 670302
Guide Price: from £4.60

Campsite,
Waterside Farm,
Edale,
Near Sheffield,
Derbyshire S30 2ZL
Tel: (0433) 70215
Guide Price: 75p per tent,
plus 75p per person

Campsite,
Mrs Hodgson,
Upper Booth Farm,
Edale,
Near Sheffield,
Derbyshire S30 2ZJ
Tel: (0433) 70250
Guide Price: £1.20 per
person

Campsite,
Coopers Camp & Caravan
Site,
Newfold Farm,
Edale,
Near Sheffield,
Derbyshire
Tel: (0433) 70372
Guide Price:

HAYFIELD

Guesthouses/B & B

The Old Bank House,
Hayfield,
Stockport,
Cheshire SK12 5EP
Tel: (0663) 747354
Guide Price: £14

Mr & Mrs G A Tier,
Bridge End Guest House,
7/9 Church Street,
Hayfield,
Stockport,
Cheshire SK12 5JE
Tel: (0663) 747321
Guide Price: £20

GLOSSOP

Norfolk Arms Hotel,
High Street West,
Glossop,
Derbyshire
Tel: (0457) 3106
Guide Price: £15

B & B,
Mr & Mrs Mills,
Birds Nest Cottage,
40 Primrose Lane,
Glossop,
Derbyshire SK13 8EW
Tel: (0457) 853478
Guide Price: £11-£12

CROWDEN

Hostel (YHA),
Peak National Park Hostel,
Crowden,
Hadfield,
Hyde,
Cheshire SK14 7HZ
Tel: (0457) 852135
Guide Price: £5.50

HOLME

Holme Castle Country Hotel,
Holme,
Holmfirth,
Huddersfield,
West Yorkshire HD7 1QG.
Tel: (0484) 686764
Guide Price: from £23.50

STANDEDGE

B & B, bunkhouse and campsite,
Mr & Mrs Mayall,
Globe Farm,
Huddersfield Road,
Standedge,
Delph,
Near Oldham,
Lancs OL3 5LU
Tel: (0457) 873040
Guide Price: from £13
Quarter of a mile from Pennine Way, map reference: 012 097. Farmhouse B & B (2 crowns) or 28-bed bunkhouse with showers &

This fine paved road over Blackstone Edge continues to puzzle the experts: is it Roman or of later origin?

drying room. Camping, provisions; meals available to all.

MARSDEN

B & B, bunkhouse and campsite,
Mrs Fussey,
Forest Farm Bunkhouse & Guest House,
Mount Road,
Marsden,
Huddersfield,
West Yorkshire HD7 6NN.
Tel: (0484) 842687
Guide Price: B & B from £9.50

BLACKSTONE EDGE

B & B, bunkhouse and campsite,
Mrs. Snelle,
Broadhead House,
Blackstone Edge,
Littleborough,
Lancs
Tel: (0706) 74686
Guide Price:

LITTLEBOROUGH

Sun Hotel,
96 Featherstall Road,
Littleborough,
Lancs
Tel: (0706) 78957
Guide Price: £15

MANKINHOLES

B & B and campsite,
Mrs Wootton,
Cross Farm,
Mankinholes,
Todmorden,
Lancs OL14 6HP
Tel: (0706) 813481
Guide Price: B & B £13, camping £1

Hostel (YHA),
Mankinholes,
Todmorden,
Lancs OL14 6HR
Tel: (0706) 812340
Guide Price: £5.50

HEBDEN BRIDGE

Guesthouses/B & Bs

Mrs Coneron,
10 Turret Royd Road,
Charlestown,
Hebden Bridge,
W Yorks HX7 6PA.
Tel: (0422) 843490

Mrs Jackson,
Old Edge,
Colden,
Hebden Bridge,
W Yorks HX7 7PG.
Tel: (0422) 844194
Guide Price: £12

Mrs Stocks,
Highgate Farm,
Hebden Bridge,
W Yorks
Tel: (0422) 842897

Prospect End,
8 Prospect Terrace,
Savile Road,
Hebden Bridge,
W Yorks HX7 6NA
Tel: (0422) 843636
Guide Price: £15
Stray Leaves,

Wadsworth,
Hebden Bridge,
W Yorks HX7 8TN
Tel: (0422) 842353
Guide Price: from £9

Mrs Love,
Height Top Farm,
Badger Lane,
Blackshaw Head,
Hebden Bridge,
W Yorks HX7 7JW
Tel: (0422) 844113
Guide Price: £11-£13

Budget

Campsite,
New Delight Inn,
Jack Bridge,
Colden,
Hebden Bridge,
W Yorks, HX7 7HT
Tel: (0422) 842795
Guide Price: 75p per person

HEPTONSTALL

B & B,
Mr & Mrs Morley,
29 Slack Top,
Heptonstall,
Hebden Bridge,
W Yorks HX7 7HA
Tel: (0422) 843636
Guide Price: £13-£15

Stoodley Pike — the distinctive landmark seen here from the burial ground in Mankinoles — was built in 1814 to commemorate peace following the Napoleonic War.

Heptonstall is a splendid hill village that's well worth exploring.

Pennine Camp & Caravan Site,
High Greenwood House,
Heptonstall,
Hebden Bridge,
W Yorks HX7 7AZ
Tel: (0422) 842287
Guide Price: from £1.50 per person

STANBURY

Old Silent Inn,
Hob Lane,
Stanbury,
Keighley,
W Yorks BD22 0HW
Tel: (0535) 42503
Guide Price: £20-£25

Guesthouses/B & Bs

Mrs Taylor,
Ponden Hall,
Stanbury,
Keighley,
W Yorks BD22 OHR,
Tel: (0535) 644154
Guide Price: £13.50

Mrs Archer,
Buckley Green,
Stanbury,
Keighley,
West Yorks BD22 OHL
Tel: (0535) 645095
Guide Price: £13

Mrs Craven,
Far Slack Farm,
Stanbury,
Keighley,
West Yorks
Tel: (0535) 642124
Guide Price: £15

Budget

**Gordon Baxter,
Upper Heights Farm,
Stanbury,
Keighley,
W Yorks BD22 OHH.
Tel: (0535) 644592 (after 6pm). Tents: £2 per person; caravan £10 per night (sleeps 3 people). Site facilities include flush toilets, H & C showers and tumble drier. On Pennine Way, just one mile from the village pub and three miles from Haworth**

COWLING

B & B,
Mrs J Sawley,
Hawthorns,
Ickornshaw,
Cowling,
Keighley,
West Yorks BD22 0DH
Tel: (0535) 633299
Guide Price: from £12

Campsite,
Mrs Hinchcliffe,
Winter House Farm,
Cowling,
Keighley,
West Yorks BD22 ONN
Tel: (0535) 632234
Guide Price: £2 per person

LOTHERSDALE

Guesthouses/B & Bs

**Mrs Brown,
Lynmouth,
Dale End,
Lothersdale,
Near Keighley,
W Yorks BD20 8EH
Tel: (0535) 632744
Guide Price: £10-£12
On Pennine Way. Washing & drying facilities; shower rooms and toilets. Camping & packed lunches.**

Mrs Wood,
Burlington House,
Lothersdale,
Via Keighley,
W Yorks
Tel: (0535) 634635
Guide Price: £12

Mrs Hardy,
Meriden,
2 Side Gate Lane,
Lothersdale,
Keighley,
West Yorks BD20 8ET
Tel: (0535) 632531
Guide Price: £13.50

Mr & Mrs Lowe,
Old Granary Cottage,
3 North View,
Lothersdale,
Near Keighley,
West Yorks BD20 8EX
Tel: (0535) 636075
Guide Price: £12.50

Campsite,
Mrs Smith,
Woodhead Farm,
Lothersdale,
Keighley,
West Yorks
Tel: (0535) 636707
Guide Price: £1 per person

EARBY

Hostel (YHA)
Glen Cottages,
Birch Hall Lane,
Earby,
Colne,
Lancs BB8 6JX
Tel: (0282) 842349
Guide Price: £3.10-£5.10

THORNTON IN CRAVEN

B & B,
Mrs Davey,
Elm Tree House,
Thornton-in-Craven,
Skipton,
North Yorks BD23 3TU
Tel: (0282) 842709
Guide Price: £11-£14.50

EAST MARTON

B & B and campsite,
Joan Pilling,
Sawley House,
East Marton,
Skipton,
North Yorks
Tel: (0282) 843207
Guide Price: B & B £12-£15

GARGRAVE

Kirk Syke Hotel,
19 High Street,
Gargrave,
Skipton,
North Yorks BD23 3RA.
Tel: (0756) 749356
Guide Price: £25

B & B,
Mrs Greenwood,
The Coppice,
31 Skipton Road,
Gargrave,
Skipton,
North Yorks BD23 3SA.
Tel: (0756) 749335
Guide Price: £10-£11

UPPER AIREDALE

Guesthouses/B & Bs

Mr & Mrs Shelmardine,
Eshton Grange,
Eshton,
Skipton,
North Yorks BD23 3QE
Tel: (0756) 749383
Guide Price: £17-£19

Mrs Philpott,
Tudor House,
Bell Busk,
Skipton,
N Yorks BD23 4DT
Tel: (07293) 301
Guide Price: £14

The remarkable limestone pavement above Malham Cove is one of the many highlights along the Pennine Way.

Mrs Robinson,
Lindon House,
Airton,
Skipton,
N Yorks BD23 4BE
Tel: (07293) 418
Guide Price: £16.50

Campsite,
Eshton Road Camp Site,
Eshton,
Skipton,
North Yorks
Tel: (0756) 749229
Guide Price: £2 per person

MALHAM

Hotels/Inns

The Buck Inn,
Malham,
Skipton,
N Yorks BD23 4DA
Tel: (07293) 317
Guide Price: £22

Mr & Mrs Oates,
Sparth House Hotel,
Malham,
Skipton,
N Yorks BD23 4DA
Tel: (07293) 315
Guide Price: £15.50-£20

Guesthouses/B & Bs

**Mrs Sharp,
Miresfield Farm,
Malham,
Skipton,
N Yorks BD23 4DA
Tel: (07293) 414
Guide Price: £16, evening meal £8. 14 rooms; en-suite rooms available. Two lounges. All home cooking.**

M Boatwright,
Beck Hall,
Malham,
Skipton,
N Yorks
Tel: (07293) 332
Guide Price: from £15

Mrs Jenkins,
Coachman's Cottage,
Hanlith,
Malham,
Skipton,
N Yorks BD24 4BP
Tel: (07293) 538
Guide Price: £15

Mrs Hargreaves,
Hanlith Hall Farm,
Hanlith,
Malham,
Skipton,
N Yorks BD23 4BP
Tel: (07293) 241
Guide Price: £13.50

Mrs Harrison,
Friars Garth,
Malham,
Skipton,
N Yorks BD23 4DB
Tel: (07293) 328
Guide Price: £9

Mr & Mrs Rawson,
Eastwood House,
Malham,
Skipton,
N Yorks BD23 4DA
Tel: (07293) 409
Guide Price: £15

Mrs Boocock,
Town End Cottage,
Malham,
Skipton,
N Yorks BD23 4DA.
Tel: (07293) 345
Guide Price: from £11

The great cliff of Malham Cove is one of the most splendid limestone features of the Yorkshire Dales.

Budget

**Bunkbarn,
Hill Top Farm,
Malham,
Skipton,
N Yorks
Tel: (07293) 320
Bunkbarn & self-catering accommodation; all rooms central heated. All enquiries to Annie & John Heseltine.**

Hostel (YHA),
John Dower Memorial Hostel,
Malham,
Skipton,
N Yorks BD23 4DE
Tel: (07293) 321
Guide Price: £6.30

Campsite,
Mr. A. Wilson,
Gordale Scar House,
Malham,
Skipton,
N Yorks BD23 4DL
Tel: (07293) 333
Guide Price: £1.50 per person

Campsite:
Mrs. Moon,
Town Head Farm,
Malham,
Skipton,
N Yorks
Tel: (07293) 310
Guide Price: from £1.50

HORTON IN RIBBLESDALE

Hotels/Inns

Mr Johnson,
The Golden Lion Hotel,
Horton-in-Ribblesdale,
Settle,
N Yorks
Tel: (07296) 206
Guide Price: £15

Mr & Mrs Hargreaves,
The Crown Inn,
Horton-in-Ribblesdale,
N Yorks BD24 OHF
Tel: (07296) 209
Guide Price: £13.70-£18.70

Guesthouses/B & Bs

Mr & Mrs Jowett,
Burnside,
Horton-in-Ribblesdale,
Settle,
N Yorks BD24 OEX
Tel: (07296) 223
Guide Price: £12-£14

Mr & Mrs Jones,
The Rowe House,
Horton-in-Ribblesdale,
Settle,
N Yorks BD24 OHT
Tel: (07296) 212
Guide Price: £16.50-£22

Mrs Kenyon,
South House Farm,
Horton-in-Ribblesdale,
Settle,
N Yorks BD24 OHU
Tel: (07296) 271
Guide Price: £11

Mr & Mrs Rhodes,
Waltergarth,
Station Road,
Horton-in-Ribblesdale,
Settle, N Yorks BD24 OHH
Tel: (07296) 221
Guide Price: £12.50

Mrs Barker,
The Willows,
Horton-in-Ribblesdale,
Settle,
N Yorks
Tel: (07296) 373
Guide Price: £12-£15

Mr & Mrs Horsfall,
Studfold House,
Horton-in-Ribblesdale,
Settle,
N Yorks
Tel: (07296) 200
Guide Price: £12

Mrs Pilkington,
Middle Studfold Farm,
Horton-in-Ribblesdale,
Settle,
N Yorks BD24 0ER
Tel: (07296) 236
Guide Price: £12

Wagi's Guest House,
Townend Cottage,
Horton-in-Ribblesdale,
Settle,
N Yorks
Tel: (07296) 320
Guide Price: from £13

Budget

Bunkhouse,
Mrs Glasgow,
Dub Cote Farm,
Horton-in-Ribblesdale,
Settle,
N Yorks
Tel: (07296)238
Guide Price: £4.50

The market town of Hawes is a welcome sight for walkers, with its pubs, cafes and plentiful accommodation.

RIBBLEHEAD

Station Inn,
Ribblehead,
Nr Ingleton,
N Yorks LA6 3AS
Tel: (05242) 41274
Guide Price: £12 (also bunkhouse barn: £4 per person)

B & B and campsite,
Mrs Timmins,
Gearstones,
Ribblehead,
Ingleton,
N Yorks LA6 3AS
Tel: (0468) 41405
Guide Price: £10.50

**B & B & bunkhouse barn,
Mrs Dorothy Smith,
Cam Houses,
Upper Langstrothdale,
Buckden,
Skipton,
N Yorks BD23 5JT
Tel: (086064) 8045
Guide Price: B & B £12,
bunkbarn £4.50 (children £3.50)**

GAYLE

B & B,
Mrs Ward,
East House,
Gayle,
Hawes,
N Yorks DL8 3RZ
Tel: (0969) 667405
Guide Price: £12

Many Pennine Way walkers consider Upper Swaledale to be one of the highlights of the whole 270 miles.

HAWES

Hotels/Inns

White Hart Inn,
Main Street,
Hawes,
N Yorks
Tel: (0969) 667259
Guide Price: £14

Herriots Hotel,
Hawes,
N Yorks
Tel: (0969) 667536
Guide Price: £21

Board Hotel,
Main Street,
Hawes,
N Yorks
Tel: (0969) 667223
Guide Price: from £14

Guesthouses/B & Bs

Mrs McGregor,
Gayle Laithe,
Gayle Lane,
Hawes,
N Yorks
Tel: (0969) 667397
Guide Price: £12

Mrs M Parker,
Dale View,
Burtersett Road,
Hawes,
N Yorks DL8 3NP
Tel: (0969) 667752
Guide Price: £11

Mrs Thwaite,
Crosby House,
Burtersett Road,
Hawes,
N Yorks DL8 3NP
Tel: (0969) 667322
Guide Price: £12

Mrs E Dunn,
Fair View,
Burtersett Road,
Hawes,
N Yorks
Tel: (0969) 667348
Guide Price: £14

Mrs Guy,
Halfway House,
Hawes,
N Yorks
Tel: (0969) 667442
Guide Price: £11

Springbank House,
Townfoot,
Hawes,
N Yorks DL8 3NW
Tel: (0969) 667376
Guide Price: £12-£14

Tarney Fors Farmhouse,
Tarney Fors,
Hawes,
N Yorks DL8 3LY
Tel: (0969) 667475
Guide Price: £13-£16

Mr & Mrs Watkinson,
Old Station House,
Hardraw Road,
Hawes,
N Yorks
Tel: (0969) 667785
Guide Price: £13.50-£15.50

Mrs Clark,
Ebor Guest House,
Burtersett Road,
Hawes,
N Yorks DL8 3NT
Tel: (0969) 667337
Guide Price: £12-£13

Mrs Andrews,
Steppe Haugh Guest House,
Town Head,
Hawes,

N Yorks
Tel: (0969) 667645
Guide Price: £12.50-£18

Budget
**Mr & Mrs Raw,
Bainbridge Ings Caravan & Camping Site,
Hawes,
N Yorks DL8 3NU
Tel: (0969) 667354
Guide Price: £1.20 per person. Camping & caravan site with shower/toilet block and constant hot water. Quiet family site — ideal for Pennine Way & Hawes.**

Hostel (YHA):
Lancaster Terrace,
Hawes,
N Yorks DL8 3LQ
Tel: (0969) 667368
Guide price: £6.30

Campsite,
Mr & Mrs Dinsdale,
Brown Moor Farm,
Hawes,
N Yorks DL8 3PS
Tel: (0969) 667338
Price on application

HARDRAW

Green Dragon Inn,
Hardraw,
Hawes,
N Yorks DL8 3LZ
Tel: (0969) 667392
Guide Price: from £16

SEDBUSK

Stone House Hotel,
Sedbusk,
Hawes,
N Yorks DL8 3PT
Tel: (0969) 667571
Guide Price: from £20

SIMONSTONE

Mrs Brenda Stott,
Shaw Ghyll Campsite,
Simonstone,
Hawes,
N Yorks DL8 3LY
Tel: (0969) 667359
Guide Price: £4 per person

THWAITE

**B & B,
Mr & Mrs Danton,
Kearton Guest House,
Thwaite,
Richmond,
N Yorks DL11 6DR
Tel: (0748) 86277
Guide Price: £15-£17**

MUKER

Campsite,
Mrs Metcalfe,
Usha Gap,
Muker,
Richmond,
N Yorks
Tel: (0748) 86214
Guide Price: £2 per night

Muker is a delightful village of stone-built cottages, surrounded by the fells of Upper Swaledale.

KELD

B & B,
Mr & Mrs Morgan,
Hilltop, Keld,
Richmond,
N Yorks DL11 6LP
Tel: (0748) 86260
Guide Price: £13.50

B & B & campsite,
Mrs Rukin,
Park Lodge, Keld,
Richmond,
N Yorks
Tel: (0748) 86274
Guide Price: B & B £13,
Camping: £1 per person

Hostel (YHA),
Keld Lodge, Keld,
Richmond,
N Yorks DL11 6LL
Tel: (0748) 86259
Guide Price: £5.50

TAN HILL

B & B and campsite,
Mrs Baines,
Tan Hill Inn,
Keld,
Richmond,
N Yorks DL11 6ED
Tel: (0833) 28246
Guide Price: B & B from £18.50

BOWES

Ancient Unicorn Inn,
Bowes,
Barnard Castle,
Co Durham DL12 9HN
Tel: (0833) 28321
Guide Price: £17.50

Guesthouses/B & Bs

Mrs Foster,
West End Farm,
Bowes,
Barnard Castle,
Co Durham DL12 9LH

Tel: (0833) 28239
Guide Price: £9
B & B and campsite,
Mrs Coleman,
Blue Cap Hall,
Stainmore Road,
Bowes,
Co Durham DL12 9RH
Tel: (0833) 28353
Guide Price: B & B £10

B & B,
Mrs Foster,
Hillandale,
Bowes,
Barnard Castle,
Co Durham
Tel: (0833) 28326
Guide Price: £9

BALDERSDALE

Hostel (YHA) and campsite,
Blackton,
Baldersdale,
Cotherstone,
Barnard Castle,
Co Durham DL12 OJZ
Tel: (0833) 50629
Guide Price: £5.50

MICKLETON

Hotel and campsite,
Rose & Crown Inn,
Mickleton,
Barnard Castle,
Co Durham DL12 OJZ
Tel: (0833) 40381
Guide Price: £1 per tent

TAN HILL INN
Britain's Highest Inn

Set in wild moorland, Tan Hill has long welcomed drovers, pack horse traders and shepherds. Today Margaret & Alec Baines offer hospitality to Pennine Way walkers, summer visitors and local farmers.

Our new extension now offers five twin en-suite rooms with TV and tea/coffee making facilities at £18.50 per person for bed & breakfast (£21.00 each for the two double rooms).

Reduced rates in winter ✷ *Bar meals in the pub*
Camping facilities available (with outside toilets)

Tan Hill Inn, Keld, Near Richmond, North Yorks DL11 6ED Tel: (0833) 28246

High Force, directly on the Pennine Way, is a spectacular waterfall — especially after rain.

MIDDLETON IN TEESDALE

Talbot Hotel,
Market Place,
Middleton in Teesdale,
Co Durham
Tel: (0833) 40273
Guide Price: £12

Guesthouses/B & Bs

Mrs Sowerby,
25 Bridge Street,
Middleton-in-Teesdale,
Co Durham DL12 OQB
Tel: (0833) 40549
Guide Price: £11

B & B and campsite,
Mrs A M Sayer,
Grassholme Farm,
Lunedale,
Middleton-in-Teesdale,
Barnard Castle,
Co Durham DL12 OPR
Tel: (0833) 40494
Guide Price: B & B £10

B & B and campsite,
Mrs Dent,
Wythes Hill Farm,
Lunedale,
Middleton-in-Teesdale,
Co Durham DL12 ONX
Tel: (0833) 40349
Guide Price: B & B £11

B & B,
Mrs Roe,
Craggsview Guest House,
13 Hill Terrace,
Middleton-in-Teesdale,
Co Durham DL12 OSL
Tel: (0833) 40798
Guide Price: £10

After visiting the village of Dufton, Pennine Way walkers have to make it over Cross Fell.

Budget

Campsite,
Daleview Caravan Park,
Middleton-in-Teesdale,
Co Durham
Tel: (0833) 40233
Guide Price: £1.75 per tent

NEWBIGGIN

Bunkhouse,
Moorhouse Farm,
Newbiggin,
Teesdale,
Barnard Castle,
Co Durham DL12 OUF
Tel: (0833) 22217
Guide Price: £2 per person

LANGDON BECK

Langdon Beck Hotel,
Forest-in-Teesdale,
Barnard Castle,
Co Durham DL12 OXP
Tel: (0833) 22267
Guide Price: £14.50-£16.50

B & B,
High Force Training Centre,
The Old Vicarage,
Langdon Beck,
Forrest-in-Teesdale,
Barnard Castle,
Co Durham DL12 OHA
Tel: (0833) 22302
Guide Price: £8.50

Budget

Hostel (YHA),
Langdon Beck Youth Hostel,
Forrest in Teesdale,
Barnard Castle,
Co Durham DL12 OXN
Tel: (0833) 22228
Guide Price: £6.30

Campsite,
Mrs Rowland,
Widdy Bank Farm,
Langdon Beck,
Forrest in Teesdale,
Barnard Castle,
Co Durham DL12 OHG
Tel: (0833) 22273
Guide Price: £1 per tent

DUFTON

Guesthouses/B & Bs

Mrs Burrows,
Bow Hall,
Dufton,
Appleby, Cumbria
Tel: (07683) 51835
Guide Price: £12.50

Mrs Howe,
Dufton Hall Farm,
Dufton,
Appleby,
Cumbria CA16 6DD
Tel: (07683) 51573
Guide Price: £12

Mrs M A Hullock,
Ghyll View,
Dufton,
Appleby,
Cumbria CA16 6DB
Tel: (07683) 51855
Guide Price: £10.50

Budget

Campsite,
Brow Farm,
Dufton,
Appleby,
Cumbria CA16 6DF
Tel: (07683) 51202
Guide Price: £1 per person

Campsite,
Silverband Park,
Silverband,
Knock,
Near Appleby,
Cumbria CA16 6DL
Tel: (07683) 61218
Guide Price: £5

Hostel (YHA),
"Redstones",
Dufton,
Appleby,
Cumbria CA16 6DB
Guide Price: £4

GARRIGILL

The George & Dragon Inn,
Garrigill,
Alston,
Cumbria CA9 3DS
Tel: (0434) 381293
Guide Price: £13 (bunkbarn £3)

Guesthouses/B & Bs

John Hardy and Wendy Foss,
Loaning Head Wholefood Vegetarian Guest House,
Garrigill,
Alston,
Cumbria
Tel: (0434) 381013
Guide Price: £13

Anne Bramwell,
Post Office,
Garrigill,
Alston,
Cumbria CA9 3DS
Tel: (0434) 381257
Guide Price: £10

ALSTON

Hotels/Inns

Victoria Inn,
Front Street,
Alston,
Cumbria CA9 3SE
Tel: (0434) 381194
Guide Price: from £11.50

The Blue Bell Inn,
Townfoot,
Alston,

Cumbria CA9 3PN
Tel: (0434)381566
Guide Price: £12.50

Guesthouses/B & Bs

Mrs Dent,
Middle Bayles Farm,
Alston,
Cumbria CA9 3BS
Tel: (0434) 381383
Guide Price: £11-£14

Mrs Lees,
Island Cottage,
Nentsberry,
Alston,
Cumbria CA9 3LW
Tel: (0434) 381860
Guide Price: £12

Budget

Campsite,
Tyne Willows Caravan Site,
Station Road,
Alston,
Cumbria CA9 3HZ
Tel: (0434) 381103
Guide Price: £1.50 per person

Hostel (YHA),
The Firs,
Alston,
Cumbria CA9 3RW
Tel: (0434) 381509
Guide Price: £4

SLAGGYFORD

Kirkstyle Inn,
Knaresdale,
Slaggyford,
Carlisle,
Cumbria CA6 7PB
Tel: (0434) 381559
Guide Price: £12.50

Guesthouses/B & Bs

Mrs Galilee,
Crianlarich,
Slaggyford,
Carlisle,
Cumbria CA6 7NJ
Tel: (0434) 381329
Guide Price: £12

Mrs Graham,
Stonehall Farm,
Slaggyford,
Carlisle,
Cumbria CA6 7PB
Tel: (0434) 381349
Guide Price: £10 (Camping £1 per person)

GREENHEAD

Greenhead Hotel,
Greenhead,
Carlisle,
Cumbria
Tel: (06977) 47411
Guide Price: from £18.50

Guesthouses/B & Bs

Pauline & Brian Staff,
Holmhead Farm,
Greenhead,
Via Carlisle,
Cumbria CA6 7HY
Tel: (0697) 47402
Guide Price: £17.50

Mrs Little,
Alloa Lea Farm,
Greenhead,
Carlisle,
Cumbria CA6 7JD
Tel: (0434) 320418
Guide Price: £1 per tent

The Roman Wall snakes over the hills from the viewpoint of Housesteads fort.

Mrs M Nolan,
The Vicarage,
Greenhead,
Carlisle,
Cumbria CA6 7HB
Tel: (06977) 47551
Guide Price: £12

Budget

Hostel (YHA),
Greenhead,
Carlisle,
Cumbria CA6 7HG
Tel: (06977) 47401
Guide Price: £5.50

Campsite,
Mr Waugh,
Roam-n-Rest Caravan Park,
Greenhead,
Carlisle,
Cumbria CA6 7HA
Tel: (06977) 47213
Guide Price: Camping £1.50 per person

Campsite,
Mrs. Scott,
Thirlwall Castle Farm,
Greenhead,
Carlisle,
Cumbria
Guide Price: 80p per person

HALTWHISTLE

Guesthouses/B & Bs

Hall Meadows,
Main Street,
Haltwhistle,
Northumberland NE49 0AZ
Tel: (0434) 321021
Guide Price: from £13

Oaky Knowe Farm,
Haltwhistle,
Northumberland NE49 0NB
Tel: (0434) 320648
Guide Price: £11-£13.50

Mr & Mrs Henderson,
Ashcroft Guest House,
Haltwhistle,

Northumberland NE49 ODA
Tel: (0434) 320313
Guide Price: £13-£15

Mrs L E Laidlow,
Whitecraig Farm,
Shield Hill,
Haltwhistle,
Northumberland NE49 9NW
Tel: (0434) 320565
Guide Price: £16

Mrs J Brown,
Broomshaw Hill Farm,
Willia Road,
Haltwhistle,
Northumberland
Tel: (0434) 320866
Guide Price: £13-£15

BARDON MILL

Hotels/Inns

Bowes Hotel,
Bardon Mill,
Hexham
Northumberland NE47 7HU
Tel: (0434) 344237
Guide Price: £12

Vallum Lodge Hotel,
Military Road,
Twice Brewed,
Near Bardon Mill,
Hexham,
Northumberland NE47 7AN
Tel: (0434) 344248
Guide Price: £19

Guesthouses/B & Bs

Mrs MacDonald,
Eldochan Hall,
Willimoteswyke,
Bardon Mill, Hexham,
Northumberland NE47 7DB
Tel: (0434) 344465
Guide Price: £14-£16

Mrs Lawson,
Winshield Farm,
Bardon Mill,
Hexham,
Northumberland
Tel: (0434) 344243
Guide Price: £11
(camping £1)

Budget

Hostel (YHA),
Once Brewed,
Military Road,
Bardon Mill,
Hexham,
Northumberland NE47 7AN
Tel: (0434) 344360
Guide Price: £4.50

HOUSESTEADS

Guesthouses/B & Bs

Mrs Huddleston,
Beggar Bog Guest House,
Housesteads,
Haydon Bridge,
Hexham,
Northumberland
Tel: (0434) 344320
Guide Price: £13

Mrs Murray,
Sewing Shields Farm,
Hadrian's Wall
(Nr Housesteads),
Haydon Bridge,
Hexham,
Northumberland NE47 6NW
Tel: (0434) 684418
Guide Price: £12

Kielder — the largest man-made forest in Europe — is skirted by Pennine Way walkers.

WARK

Guesthouses/B & Bs

Mrs Nichol,
Hetherington,
Wark,
Hexham,
Northumberland NE48 3DR
Tel: (0434) 230260
Guide Price: £10

Anne Hutchinson,
The Haining,
Near Stonehaugh,
Wark,
Hexham,
Northumberland NE48 3ED
Tel: (0434) 230680
Guide Price: £12

Budget

Campsite and bunkhouse,
Mrs F Thompson,
Horneystead, Wark,
Hexham,
Northumberland
Tel: (0660) 230689
Guide Price: £1 per person

BELLINGHAM

Hotels/Inns

Riverdale Hall Hotel,
Bellingham,
Hexham,
Northumberland
Tel: (0434) 220254
Guide Price: £24
The only hotel in Northumberland with RAC merit award for its food. Large indoor pool, all bedrooms en-suite. Periphery of National Park; Pennine Way passes alongside.

The Cheviot Hotel,
Bellingham,
Hexham,
Northumberland
Tel: (0434) 220216
Guide Price: £18.50

Guesthouses/B & Bs

Lyndale,
Bellingham,
Hexham,

Northumberland NE48 2AW
Tel: (0434) 220361
Guide Price: £13-£16

Mrs Batey,
Lynn View,
Bellingham,
Hexham,
Northumberland NE48 2BL
Tel: (0434) 220344
Guide Price: £12

Mr & Mrs Minchin,
Westfield House,
Bellingham,
Hexham,
Northumberland NE48 2DP
Tel: (0434) 220340
Price Guide: £16

Mrs Young,
Victoria House,
Bellingham,
Hexham,
Northumberland
Tel: (0434) 220229
Guide Price: £10

Mr & Mrs Gaskin,
Lyndale Guest House,
Bellingham,
Hexham,
Northumberland NE48 2AW
Tel: (0434) 220361
Guide Price: £12

Budget

Hostel (YHA),
Woodburn Road,
Bellingham,
Hexham,
Northumberland NE48 2ED
Tel: (0660) 20313
Guide Price: £3.20

Campsite,
T & K Telfar,
Demeane Farm,
Bellingham,
Hexham,
Northumberland
Tel: (0434) 220258
Guide Price: (£1.50 per person)

BYRNESS

Guesthouses/B & B,

Mrs Henderson,
10 Otterburn Green,
Byrness,
Otterburn,
Newcastle upon Tyne
NE19 1TS
Tel: (0830) 20604
Guide Price: £11

Mrs Anderson,
4 South Green,
Byrness,
Otterburn,
Newcastle upon Tyne
NE19 1TT
Tel: (0830) 20653
Guide Price: £8.50

Budget

Hostel (YHA),
7 Otterburn Green,
Byrness,
Otterburn,
Newcastle upon Tyne
NE19 1TS
Tel: (0830) 20222
Guide Price: £5.10

Campsite, bunkhouse and B & B,
Byrness Caravan Park,
Cottonshopeburn Foot,
Near Otterburn,
Northumberland
Tel: (0830) 20259
Guide Price: Camping from £2.50 per person

CHEVIOTS

Guesthouses/B & Bs

Mrs Bleming,
Blindburn Farm,
Harbottle,
Morpeth,
Northumberland NE65 7DD
Tel: (0669) 50202
Guide Price: £8

B & B and camping,
Mrs Buglass,
Uswayford,
Harbottle,
Morpeth,
Northumberland NE65 7BU
Tel: (0669) 50237
Guide Price: £10, camping £2

B & B and camping,
Mrs Johnson,
Belford on Bowmont,
Yetholm,
Kelso,
Roxburghshire
Tel: (057) 382362
Guide Price: £11, camping £2 per person.

KIRK YETHOLM

Hotels/Inns

Border Hotel,
Woodmarket,
Kelso,
Roxburghshire
Tel: (0573) 24791
Guide Price: £12

The Border Hotel,
Kirk Yetholm,
Kelso,
Roxburghshire
Tel: (057) 382237
Guide Price: £15

Guesthouses/B & Bs

Valleydene Guest House,
Kirk Yetholm,
Kelso,
Roxburghshire
Tel: (057) 382286
Guide Price: £12

Budget

Hostel (SYHA),
Kirk Yetholm,
Kelso,
Roxburghshire
Tel: (057) 382631
Guide Price: £3.45-£4.20

COAST to COAST WALK

The Coast to Coast Walk is the creation of the late Alfred Wainwright, who was responsible — through his wonderfully detailed, hand-written books — for introducing many people to the pleasures of fell-walking and the great outdoors.

While the Pennine Way goes basically north to south, the Coast to Coast path is orientated east to west. The Pennine Way has "official" starting and finishing points, but the Coast to Coast, as its name indicates, is even more definitive: you couldn't walk any further if you tried. Not without getting your feet wet anyway...

In his book *A Coast to Coast Walk*, Wainwright recommends tackling the route from west to east. This entails a start at St Bees Head in Cumbria and a finish, some 190 miles later, at the picturesque little fishing village of Robin Hood's Bay, on the North Yorkshire coast.

Between these sea cliffs can be found some of the finest walking country in the North — emphasised by the fact that two-thirds of the walk traverses national parks: Lake District, Yorkshire Dales and the North York Moors. The Lakeland section comprises a spectacular landscape of high peaks and mountain passes; there can be few hostels that occupy such a splendid and remote site as the Black Sail Hut in Ennerdale, accessible only to pedestrians.

A break in the clouds allows a ray of sun to light up a hillside in Swaledale.

The walk continues through the steep-sided valley of Swaledale, which offers splendid walking and perhaps the best views in the Yorkshire Dales. After calling in at Richmond, the route crosses the Vale of Mowbray and the Cleveland Hills, until Robin Hoods Bay is sighted.

Wainwright recommended allowing a fortnight to complete the walk and really enjoy the countryside. The more athletic could do it in half the time, but what's the hurry?

The walk tends to avoid towns; Richmond, in North Yorkshire, is the exception, and that is by design, since it's such a splendid place to explore. Nevertheless, there are plenty of "bed and breakfasts" on the route, and youth hostellers are well served too. Many tourist information centres (see Appendix) operate an accommodation booking service.

Walkers with two weeks to spare for the walk may wish to consider dividing it into the following stages, with daily mileage in brackets:

St Bees to Ennerdale Bridge (14)
Ennerdale Bridge to Rosthwaite (14)
Rosthwaite to Grasmere (9)
Grasmere to Patterdale (8)
Patterdale to Shap (16)
Shap to Kirkby Stephen (20)
Kirkby Stephen to Keld (12)
Keld to Reeth (11)
Reeth to Richmond (10)
Richmond to Ingleby Cross (23)
Ingleby Cross to Clay Bank Top (12)
Clay Bank Top to Blakey (9)
Blakey to Grosmont (12)

St. Bees Head
IRISH SEA
Whitehaven
Ennerdale Bridge
Rosthwaite
Grasmere
Patterdale
Shap
Kirkby Stephen
Keld
eld
Reeth
Richmond
Danby Wiske
Ingleby Cross
Clay Bank Top
Glaisdale
Whitby
Robin Hoods Bay
Scarborough
NORTH SEA

ST BEES

Hotels/Inns

Queens Hotel,
Main Street,
St Bees, Cumbria CA27 0DE
Tel: (0946) 822287
Guide Price £15.50

Manor House Inn,
11/12 Main Street,
St Bees,
Cumbria CA27 0DE
Tel: (0946) 822425
Guide Price: £15

Guesthouses/B & Bs

**Mrs E M Smith,
Stonehouse Farm,
Near Railway Station,
Main Street,
St Bees,
Cumbria CA27 0DE
Tel: (0946) 822224
Guide Price: £12-£16
Comfortable modernised Georgian farmhouse; all amenities including CH & CTV. On the Coast to Coast route and near shops and pubs; warm welcome.**

**Miss A King,
Alpha House,
1, Richmond Crescent,
St Bees,
Cumbria CA27 0EP
Tel: (0946) 822424
Guide Price: £8.50-£11
Home cooking — conventional or vegetarian — and packed lunches by prior request. Flasks filled. Situated at start of Coast to Coast walk. Open all year.**

Mrs Moffatt,
Outrigg House,
St Bees,
Cumbria CA27 0AN
Tel: (0946) 822348
Guide Price: £12-£13

Mr & Mrs Pearson,
Kinder How Guest House,
St Bees,
Cumbria CA27 0AS
(0946) 822376
Guide Price: £14

Mrs Sharpe,
4 Victoria Terrace,
St Bees,
Cumbria CA27 0EL
(0946) 822583
Guide Price: £14-£18

Mr & Mrs Durber,
3 Richmond Crescent,
St Bees,
Cumbria CA27 0EP
Tel: (0946) 822313
Guide Price: £11-£16

Mrs Jones,
Penrhyn Villa,
75 Main Street,
St Bees,
Cumbria CA27 0AL
Tel: (0946) 822423
Guide Price: £10

Mr & Mrs Milligan,
Khandhalla,
High House Road,
St Bees CA27 0BV
Tel: (0946) 822377
Guide Price: £10

Mrs Whitehead,
Tomlin Guest House,
Beach Road,
St Bees CA27 0EN
Tel: (0946) 822284
Guide Price: £11-£13

Mrs Noble,
1, Victoria Terrace,
Abbey Road,
St Bees CA27 0EL
Tel: (0946) 822597
Guide Price: £10.50

Budget

Campsite,
Beachcomber Park,
Beach Road,
St Bees,
Cumbria CA27 0ES
Tel: (0946) 822777
Guide Price: £4 per tent

SANDWITH

B & B,
Mrs Day,
Alkbank Cottage,
Sandwith,
Cumbria CA28 9UG
Tel: (0946) 695771
Guide Price: £10

CLEATOR

Guesthouses/B & Bs

Mrs Fowler,
3 Cleator Gate,
Cleator,
Cumbria CA23 3DN
Tel: (0946) 813394
Guide Price: £12

Mrs Bradshaw,
Inglenook Cottage,
37 Main Street,
Cleator,
Cumbria CA23 3BU
Tel: (0946) 813156
Guide Price: £10

ENNERDALE

Shepherd's Arms Hotel,
Ennerdale Bridge,
Cleator CA23 3AR
Tel: (0946) 861249
Guide Price £17.50-£19

Guesthouses/B & Bs

Mrs Sterland,
Brookside,
Ennerdale,
Cumbria CA23 3AR
Tel: (0946) 861470
Guide Price: £12

Mrs Loxham,
Beckfoot Farm,
Ennerdale,
Cumbria CA23 3AU
Tel: (0946) 861235
Guide Price: £12.50-£14

Mrs H Hind,
Low Moor End Farm,
Ennerdale,
Cleator,
Cumbria CA23 3AS
Tel: (0946) 861388
Guide Price: £12.50-£15

Budget

Hostel (YHA),
Cat Crag,
Ennerdale, Cleator,
Cumbria CA23 3AX
Tel: (0946) 861237
Guide Price: £3.50-£5.50

Campsite,
Mrs P A Humphreys,
High Bridge Farm,
Ennerdale, Cleator,
Cumbria CA23 3AR
Tel: (0946) 861339
Guide Price: £1.50 per person

Hostel (YHA),
Black Sail Hut,
Ennerdale, Cleator,
Cumbria CA12 5XG
Guide Price: £2.60

ESKDALE

B & B,
Stanley Ghyll House,
Boot Holmbrook,
Eskdale CA19 1TF
Tel: (09403) 327
Guide Price: £17

BUTTERMERE

Guesthouses/B & Bs

**Mr & Mrs Knight,
Trevene,
Buttermere,
Cockermouth
Cumbria CA13 9XA
Tel: (059685) 210
Guide Price: £12
Two hundred yards from village on Wainwright's picturesque alternative route. Open all year. Two nearby hotels serve bar meals. Packed lunches available and flasks filled.**

Rannerdale Farm,
Buttermere,
Cockermouth,
Cumbria CA13 9UY
Tel: (059685) 232
Guide Price: £12

B & B and campsite,
Dalegarth,
Buttermere,
Cockermouth,
Cumbria CA13 9XA
Tel: (059685) 233
Guide Price: £11-£15.50

BORROWDALE

Hotels/Inns

Langstrath Hotel,
Stonethwaite,
Borrowdale,
Keswick,
Cumbria CA12 5XG
Tel: (07687) 77239
Guide Price: £25

Scafell Hotel,
Rosthwaite,
Borrowdale,
Keswick,
Cumbria CA12 5XB
Tel: (0768) 784208
Guide Price: £26.50

Guesthouses/B & Bs

Mr & Mrs Jackson,
Knotts View Guest House,
Stonethwaite,
Borrowdale,
Cumbria CA12 5XG
Tel: (07687) 77604
Guide Price: £14

Mrs Jackson,
Nook Farm,
Rosthwaite,
Borrowdale,
Cumbria CA12 5XB
Tel: (07687) 77677
Guide Price: £13

Yew Craggs Guest House,
Rosthwaite,
Borrowdale,
Cumbria
Tel: (07687) 260
Guide Price: from £13

Grasmere is one of the loveliest stretches of water in the whole of the Lake District.

Mrs Relph,
Oak Cottage,
Rosthwaite, Cumbria
Tel: (07687) 77236
Guide Price: £12

Mrs Brownlee,
Stonethwaite Farm,
Stonethwaite,
Borrowdale,
Cumbria CA12 5XG
Tel: (07687) 77234
Guide Price: £12

Mrs Dunckley,
Gillercombe,
Stonethwaite Road End,
Rosthwaite,
Borrowdale,
Cumbria CA12 5XG
Tel: (07687) 77602
Guide Price: £11

Glaramara,
Seatoller,
Borrowdale,
Keswick,
Cumbria CA12 5XQ
Tel: (095684) 222
Guide Price: £10.50

Budget

Stonethwaite Farm Campsite,
Borrowdale,
Keswick,
Cumbria CA12 5XG
Tel: (059684) 234
Guide Price: £3 per tent

GRASMERE

Guesthouses/B & Bs

Mrs Higgins,
Ash Cottage Guest House,
Red Lion Square,
Grasmere,
Cumbria LA22 9SP
Tel: (09665) 224
Guide Price: from £23

Lake View Guest House,
Lake View Drive,
Grasmere,
Cumbria LA22 9TD
Tel: (09665) 384
Guide Price: £18

Mrs Clark,
Banerigg,
Lake Road,
Grasmere,
Cumbria LA22 9PW
Tel: (09665) 204
Guide Price: £16

Mr Smith,
Dunmail Guest House,
Grasmere,
Cumbria LA22 9RE
Tel: (09665) 256
Guide Price: £14.50

Forest Side,
Grasmere LA22 9RN
Tel: (09665) 250
Guide Price: £17

Mrs Nelson,
Undercrag,
Easedale Road,
Grasmere,
Cumbria LA22 9QD
Tel: (09665) 349
Guide Price: £15-£18

GLENRIDDING

Guesthouses/B & Bs

Mrs Beaty,
Home Farm,
Glenridding,
Patterdale,
Penrith,
Cumbria CA11 0PU
Tel: (07684) 82370
Guide Price: £11

Mrs Pool,
Beech House,
Glenridding,
Penrith,
Cumbria CA11 0PA
Tel: (07684) 82339
Guide Price: £12

Mr & Mrs Bevan,
Graystones,
Beckside,
Glenridding,
Penrith,
Cumbria CA11 0PA
Tel: (07684) 82393
Guide Price: £12.50

Ullswater and Glenridding: lake and village in a splendidly craggy setting.

Budget
Gillside Campsite,
Glenridding,
Penrith,
Cumbria CA11 0QQ
Tel: (07684) 82346
Guide Price: £1.80

PATTERDALE

White Lion Inn,
Patterdale,
Penrith,
Cumbria CA11 0NW
Tel: (07684) 82214
Guide Price: from £16.50

The Patterdale Hotel,
Patterdale,
Penrith,
Cumbria CA11 0NN
Tel: (07684) 82231
Guide Price: £20

Guesthouses/B & Bs
Mrs Halliday,
Beckstones,
Patterdale,
Penrith,
Cumbria CA11 0NP
Tel: (07684) 82584
Guide Price: £13

Mrs Barker,
Noran Bank Farm,
Patterdale,
Penrith,
Cumbria CA11 0NR
Tel: (07684) 82201
Guide Price: £11.50

Mrs Knight,
Fellside,
Hartsop,
Patterdale,
Penrith,
Cumbria CA11 0NZ
Tel: (07684) 82532
Guide Price: £14

Budget
Hostel (YHA),
Goldrill House,
Patterdale, Penrith,
Cumbria CA11 0NW
Tel: (08532) 394
Guide Price: £5

BROTHERSWATER

Bunkhouse,
Sykeside Holiday Park,
Brotherswater,
Penrith,
Cumbria CA11 0NZ
Tel: (07684) 82239
Guide Price: £1.50

BAMPTON GRANGE

Crown & Mitre,
Bampton Grange,
Penrith,
Cumbria CA10 2QR
Tel: (09313) 225
Guide Price: £14

Guesthouses/B & Bs
Mrs Weide,
Grange Farm,
Bampton Grange,
Penrith,
Cumbria CA10 2QR
Tel: (09313) 263
Guide Price: £10

Leyton Barn,
Bampton Grange,
Penrith,
Cumbria CA10 2QR
Tel: (09313) 314
Guide Price: £8

BAMPTON

Hotels/Inns

Haweswater Hotel,
Bampton,
Penrith,
Cumbria
Tel: (09313) 235
Guide Price: £22-£25

St Patrick's Well Inn,
Bampton,
Penrith,
Cumbria
Tel: (09313) 244
Guide Price: £13.50

HELTON

B & B,
Mrs White,
Beckfoot House,
Helton,
Penrith,
Cumbria CA10 2QB
Tel: (09313) 241
Guide Price: from £20

SHAP

Hotels/Inns

Crown Inn,
Shap,
Penrith,
Cumbria CA10 3ML
Tel: (09316) 229
Guide Price: £15

Bull Head Inn,
Shap,
Penrith,
Cumbria CA10 3NG
Tel: (09316) 678
Guide Price: £15

Kings Arms Hotel,
Main Street,
Shap,
Penrith,
Cumbria CA10 3NU
Tel: (09316) 277
Guide Price: £15

Guesthouses/B & Bs

Mrs Kirkby,
New Ing Farm,
Shap,
Penrith,
Cumbria CA10 3LX
Tel: (09316) 661
Guide Price: from £10

K & V Farmer,
Fell House,
Shap,
Penrith,
Cumbria CA10 3NY
Tel: (09316) 343
Guide Price: £10

Mrs Ryland,
Pleasant View,
Shap,
Penrith,
Cumbria CA10 3PD
Tel: (09316) 336
Guide Price: £11

K & V Farmer,
Fell House,
Shap,
Penrith,
Cumbria CA10 3NY
Tel: (09316) 343
Guide Price: £12

ORTON

George Hotel,
Orton,
Cumbria CA10 3JR
Tel: (05874) 229
Guide Price: £15

Kirkby Stephen — once a busy stage-coach halt — is now a favourite haunt of walkers.

Guesthouses/B & Bs

Mrs Dunford,
Berwyn House,
Orton,
Cumbria CA10 3RQ
Tel: (05874) 345
Guide Price: £12

Mrs Winder,
New House Farm,
Raisbeck,
Orton,
Cumbria
Tel: (05874) 324
Guide Price: £10-£12

NEWBIGGIN ON LUNE

Guesthouses/B & Bs

B & B and campsite,
Mrs D Ousby,
Bents Farm,
Newbiggin-on-Lune,
Kirkby Stephen,
Cumbria CA17 4NX
Tel: (05873) 681
Guide Price: B & B £10, camping £2 per person.

Mrs B Boustead,
Tranna Hill,
Newbiggin-on-Lune,
Kirkby Stephen,
Cumbria CA17 4NY
Tel: (05873) 227
Guide Price: £10.50

Mrs Young,
Church View Farmhouse,
Newbiggin-on-Lune,
Kirkby Stephen,
Cumbria CA17 4NS
Tel: (05873) 283
Guide Price: £11

SOULBY

Guesthouses/B & Bs

Mrs A E March,
Hutton Lodge,
Soulby,
Kirkby Stephen,
Cumbria CA17 4PL
Tel: (07683) 71396
Guide Price: £12-£14

Mrs Sayer,
Syke Side Farm,
Soulby,
Kirkby Stephen,
Cumbria CA17 4PJ
Tel: (07683) 71137
Guide Price: £9

The Old Vicarage,
Soulby,
Kirkby Stephen
Cumbria CA17 4PL
Tel: (07683) 71477
Guide Price: £13

KIRKBY STEPHEN

Hotels/Inns

Croglin Castle Hotel,
South Road,
Kirkby Stephen,
Cumbria CA17 4SY
Tel: (07683) 71389
Guide Price: £12

Black Bull Hotel,
Kirkby Stephen,
Cumbria CA17 4QN
Tel: (07683) 71237
Guide Price: £13

Town Head House,
High Street,
Kirkby Stephen,
Cumbria CA17 4SH
Tel: (07683) 71044
Guide Price: £34

Guesthouse/B & Bs,

Mrs Claxton,
The Old Court House,
High Street,

Pennine View Caravan Park
Station Road, Kirkby Stephen, Cumbria CA17 4SZ

Tel: (07683) 71717

Pennine View Caravan Park is one mile south of the town centre. Newly-built toilet block with hot showers and full laundry facilities. Public house close by with good meals and traditional ales. Camping: £2 per person. Map reference: 772075. For brochure contact Mrs S Sim.

Even after the peaks and passes of Lakeland, Coast to Coast walkers will not be disappointed by Swaledale.

Kirkby Stephen,
Cumbria CA17 4SH
Tel: (07683) 71061
Guide Price: £12.50-£20

Jolly Farmer's Guest House,
63 High Street,
Kirkby Stephen,
Cumbria CA17 4SH
Tel: (07683) 71063
Guide Price: £12.50

Mrs Crowson,
Sower Pow,
Victoria Square,
Kirkby Stephen,
Cumbria CA17 4QA
Tel: (07683) 71030
Guide Price: £12.50

Mrs Robinson,
Barium House,
Nateby Road,
Kirkby Stephen,
Cumbria
Tel: (07683) 71095
Guide Price: £12

Mrs Prime,
Redmayne House,
Silver Street,
Kirkby Stephen,
Cumbria CA17 4RB
Tel: (07683) 71441
Guide Price: £12.50

Mrs Bradwell,
Fletcher House,
Kirkby Stephen,
Cumbria CA17 4QQ
Tel: (07683) 71013
Guide Price: £15

Mrs Sue Rogan,
Standards Villa,
South Road,
Kirkby Stephen,
Cumbria CA17 4SN
Tel: (07683) 72138
Guide Price: from £12

Annedd Gwyon,
46 High Street,
Kirkby Stephen,
Cumbria CA17 4SH
Tel: (07683) 72302
Guide Price: £12-15

Winton Manor Farmhouse,
Winton,
Kirkby Stephen,
Cumbria CA17 4ML
Tel: (07683) 71255
Guide Price: £12.50

Mr & Mrs Hughes,
Redenol House,
56 South Road,
Kirkby Stephen,
Cumbria CA17 4SN
Tel: (07683) 71489
Guide Price: £12

Budget

Campsite,
Pennine View Caravan Park,
Station Road,
Kirkby Stephen,
Cumbria CA17 4SZ
Tel: (07683) 71717
Guide Price: £2 per person

Hostel (YHA),
Fletcher Hill,
Market Street,
Kirkby Stephen,
Cumbria CA17 4QQ
Guide Price: from £4

KELD

Guesthouses/B & Bs

Mr & Mrs Morgan,
Hilltop,
Keld,
Richmond,
N Yorks DL11 6LP
Tel: (0748) 86260
Guide Price: £13.50

B & B and campsite,
Mrs Rukin,
Park Lodge,
Keld,
Richmond,
N Yorks
Tel: (0748) 86274
Guide Price: B & B £13,
Camping: £1 per person

THWAITE

B & B,
Mr & Mrs Danton,

The steep-sided ravine of Gunnerside Gill was one of the main lead-mining sites in Swaledale.

**Kearton Guest House,
Thwaite,
Richmond,
N Yorks DL11 6DR
Tel: (0748) 86277
Guide Price: £15-17**

MUKER

Usha Gap Camp & Caravan Site,
Usha Gap,
Muker,
Richmond,
N Yorks
Tel: (0748) 86214
Guide Price: £2 per person

GUNNERSIDE

Guesthouses/B & Bs

Rogans Country House,
Satron,
Gunnerside,
Near Richmond,
N Yorks DL11 6JW
Tel: (0748) 86414
Guide Price: £17

Mrs Porter,
Oxnop Hall,
Low Oxnop,
Richmond,
N Yorks DL11 6JJ
Tel: (0748) 86253
Guide Price: £13-£17

LOW ROW

Punch Bowl Hotel,
Low Row,
Richmond,
N Yorks DL11 6PS
Tel: (0748) 86233
Guide Price: from £15
(bunkhouse £3)

Guesthouses/B & Bs

Ann Chamberlain,
Rowleth End,
Low Row,
Richmond,
N Yorks DL11 6PY
Tel: (0748) 86327
Guide Price: £14

Mr Earl,
Peat Gate Head Guest House,
Low Row,
Near Richmond,
N Yorks DL11 6PP
Tel: (0748) 86388
Guide Price: £19.50

Mrs Elgar,
Crackpot Cottage,
Crackpot,
Low Row,
Richmond,
N Yorks DL11 6NW
Tel: (0748) 86486
Guide Price: £12.50-£13.50

ARKENGARTHDALE

B & B,
Mr & Mrs Whitworth,
The White House,
Arkle Town,
Arkengarthdale,
N Yorks DL11 6RB
Tel: (0748) 84203
Guide Price: £12.50-£15

REETH

Hotels/Inns

Burgoyne Hotel,
Reeth,
Richmond,
N Yorks DL11 6SN
Tel: (0748) 84292
Guide Price: £17.50

Black Bull Hotel,
Reeth,
Richmond,
N Yorks
Tel: (0748) 84213
Guide Price: £14-£15

Kings Arms Hotel,
High Row,
Reeth,
Richmond,
N Yorks DL11 6SY
Tel: (0748) 84259
Guide Price: £13.50

Guesthouses/B & Bs

Mrs Hodgson,
Hackney House,
Reeth,
Richmond,
N Yorks DL11 6TW
Tel: (0748) 84302
Guide Price: £12

Mrs Peacock,
Elder Peak,
Arkengarthdale Road,
Reeth,
Richmond,
N Yorks DL11 6QZ
Tel: (0748) 84770
Guide Price: £10

Mrs Davis,
2 Bridge Terrace,
Reeth,
Richmond,
N Yorks DL11 6TP
Tel: (0748) 84572
Guide Price: £11.50

Mr Hodgson,
Kernot Court,
Reeth,
Richmond,
N Yorks DL11 6SF
Tel: (0748) 84662
Guide Price: from £8

Mrs Archer,
Hilary House,
Reeth,
Richmond,
N Yorks DL11 6TG
Tel: (0748) 84507
Guide Price: £12.50

Mrs Bain,
Walpardoe,
Anvil Square,
Reeth,
Richmond,
N Yorks DL11 6TE
Tel: (0748) 84626
Guide Price: £11.50

Mrs Bailey,
Fremington Mill Farm,
Reeth,
Richmond,
N Yorks DL11 6AR
Tel: (0748) 84581
Guide Price: £12-£13

Mrs Dolphin,
Ewell,
Arkengarthdale Road,
Reeth,
Richmond,
N Yorks DL11 6SQ
Tel: (0748) 84406
Guide Price: £11-£13

GRINTON

The Bridge Hotel,
Grinton,
Richmond,
N Yorks DL11 6HH
Tel: (0748) 84224
Guide Price: £17.50

B & B,
Mrs Hinson,
The Smithy,
Grinton,
Richmond,

Richmond still keeps its essentially medieval layout, with cobbled market-place — seen here from the castle keep.

N Yorks DL11 6HJ
Tel: (0748) 84454
Guide Price: £10

Hostel (YHA),
Grinton Lodge,
Grinton,
Richmond,
N Yorks DL11 6HS
Tel: (0748) 84206
Guide Price: £5.80

MARRICK

Guesthouses/B & Bs

Mrs Sutcliffe,
Helmsley House,
Marrick,
Richmond,
N Yorks DL11 7LQ
Tel: (0748) 84351
Guide Price: £12-£13

S M Bainbridge,
Marrick Abbey Farm,
Marrick,
Richmond,
N Yorks DL11 7LD
Tel: (0748) 84734
Guide Price: £10

RICHMOND

Hotels/Inns

Turf Hotel,
Victoria Road, Richmond,
N Yorks DL10 4DW
Tel: (0748) 2673
Guide Price: £15

Black Lion Hotel,
Finkle Street, Richmond,
N Yorks DL10 4QH
Tel: (0748) 3121
Guide Price: £16

Mr & Mrs Elliott,
The Buck Inn, Newbiggin,
Richmond DL10 4DX
Tel: (0748) 2259
Guide Price: £12

Guesthouses/B & Bs

Mrs Dalton,
Fieldview Guest House,
15 Queens Road,
Richmond,
N Yorks DL10 4AJ
Tel: (0748) 825866
Guide Price: £13-£17

Mr & Mrs Park,
Pottergate Guest House,
Pottergate,
Richmond,
N Yorks DL10 4AB
Tel: (0748) 823826
Guide Price: £12-£15

Mrs Giles,
Oglethorpe House,
Pottergate,
Richmond,
N Yorks DL10 4AB
Tel: (0748) 823168
Guide Price: £12.50

Mr & Mrs Jackson,
Willance House,
24 Frenchgate,
Richmond,
N Yorks DL10 7AG
Tel: (0748) 824467
Guide Price: £15

Mrs Gibson,
West Cottage,
Victoria Road,
Richmond,
N Yorks DL10 4AS
Tel: (0748) 824046
Guide Price: £12.50-£15

Ridgeway Guest House,
47 Darlington Road,
Richmond,
N Yorks DL10 4BG
Tel: (0748) 823801
Guide Price: £17

West End Guest House,
45 Reeth Road,
Richmond,
N Yorks DL10 4EX
Tel: (0748) 824783
Guide Price: £14

Mrs Pepper,
Windsor House,
9 Castle Hill,
Richmond,
N Yorks DL10 4QP
Tel: (0748) 823285
Guide Price: £12

Mrs Guile,
Emmanuel Guest House,
41 Maison Dieu,
Richmond,
N Yorks DL10 7AU
Tel: (0748) 823584
Guide Price: £11

Mrs M Irwin,
Hillcrest, Sleegill,
Richmond,
N Yorks DL10 4RH
Tel: (0748) 823280
Guide Price: £12

Mr & Mrs Prees,
47 Maison Dieu,
Richmond,
N Yorks DL10 7AU
Tel: (0748) 825982
Guide Price: £11

Mrs Dick,
Station House,
Richmond,
N Yorks DL10 4LE
Tel: (0748) 823320
Guide Price: £12

Mrs Hartwell,
Dalesend Guest House,
Richmond,
N Yorks DL10 4EH
Tel: (0748) 825998
Guide Price: £11

Budget

Campsite,
Swaleview Caravan Park,
Reeth Road, Richmond,
N Yorks
Tel: (0748) 823106
Guide Price: from £2.10

BROMPTON ON SWALE

The Tudor Hotel,
Gatherley Road,
Brompton-on-Swale,
Richmond,
N Yorks DL10 7JF
Tel: (0748) 818021
Guide Price: £22.50

Guesthouses/B & Bs

The Oast House,
10 Richmond Road,
Brompton-on-Swale,
Richmond,
N Yorks DL10 7HE
Tel: (0748) 818483
Guide Price: £14-£16

Broken Brae Crossing Cottage,
Richmond Road,
Brompton-on-Swale,
Richmond,
N Yorks DL10 7EY
Tel: (0748) 2307
Guide Price: from £9

CATTERICK BRIDGE

Bridge House Hotel,
Catterick Bridge,
Richmond,
N Yorks DL10 7PE
Tel: (0748) 818331
Guide Price: from £21

B & B, Mrs Peacock,
Thornborough Farm,
Catterick Bridge,
Richmond,
N Yorks DL10 7PQ
Tel: (0748) 811421
Guide Price: £15

Restaurant, bar meals lunch & evening,
Beer garden
Rooms with Satellite TV, telephone,
tea & coffee making facilities
Single rooms from £25
Double rooms from £40

Proprietors: Andrew & Jennifer Ridgway

Catterick Bridge, Richmond
North Yorkshire DL10 7PE
Tel: (0748) 818331

CATTERICK VILLAGE

Angel Inn,
19 High Street,
Catterick Village,
Nr Richmond,
N Yorks DL10 7LL
Tel: (0748) 818490
Guide Price: £17

B & B,
Mr & Mrs McGillivray,
Rose Cottage Guest House,
26 High Street,
Catterick Village,
Richmond,
N Yorks DL10 7LJ
Tel: (0748) 811164
Guide Price: from £22.50

SCORTON

B & B,
Mrs M Thompson,
Leylands Farm,
Ellerton-on-Swale,
Scorton,
Richmond,
N Yorks
Guide Price: £12

BOLTON-ON-SWALE

Guesthouses/B & Bs

**Mrs Thompson,
Leylands Farm,
Bolton-on-Swale,
Richmond,
N Yorks DL10 6AJ
Tel: (0748) 811491
Guide Price: B & B £12; bunkroom & breakfast £9; camping £2. On Coast to Coast walk: map ref: 262 987. B & B and bunk bedroom; breakfast & evening meal. Camping, with washroom & shower.**

STREETLAM

B & B,
Mrs Robertshaw,
Middle Brockholme Farm,
Streetlam,
Northallerton,
N Yorks DL7 0AJ
Tel: (0609) 780456
Guide Price: £12

DANBY WISKE

The White Swan Inn,
Danby Wiske,
Northallerton,
N Yorks DL7 0NQ
Tel: (0609) 770122
Guide Price: £12.50
(camping: £1 per person)

B & B,
Mrs Astbury,
Glebe House,
Danby Wiske,
Northallerton,
N Yorks DL7 0LY
Tel: (0609) 775546
Guide Price: £10

OAK TREE HILL

B & B and camping,
Mrs Pearson,
Lovesome Hill Farm,
Lovesome Hill,
Northallerton,
N Yorks DL6 2PB
Tel: (0609) 772311
Guide Price: B & B £12.50-£15

Bob & Merlyn Watson

The White Swan

Danby Wiske

NORTHALLERTON
NORTH YORKS DL7 0NQ
Tel: (0609) 770122

BED & BREAKFAST ✷ BAR MEALS ✷ FREE HOUSE
✷ OVERNIGHT CAMPING ✷

INGLEBY CROSS

Blue Bell Inn,
(and camping),
Ingleby Cross,
Northallerton,
N Yorks DL6 3NF
Tel: (0609) 82272
Guide Price: £11.50

Guesthouses/B & Bs

Mrs Christon, Elstavale,
Ingleby Arncliffe,
Northallerton,
N Yorks DL6 3LZ
Tel: (0609) 82302
Guide Price: £11

Mrs Backhouse,
Monks House,
Ingleby Arncliffe,
Northallerton,
N Yorks DL6 3ND
Tel: (0609) 82294
Guide Price: £12

North York Moors
Adventure Centre,
Park House, Ingleby Cross,
Near Osmotherley,
Northallerton,
N Yorks DL6 3PE
Tel: (0609) 82571
Guide Price: £10 (camping
50p)

Mrs Hillary,
Ox-Hill Farm,
Ingleby Cross,
Northallerton,
N Yorks DL6 3NJ
Tel: (0609) 82255
Guide Price: £11

OSMOTHERLEY

**Queen Catherine Hotel,
7 West End,
Osmotherley,
Northallerton,
N Yorks DL6 3AG
Tel: (0609) 83209
Family-run pub/hotel,
£16.50 with full breakfast.
Rooms warm & comfortable
with tea & coffee facilities
(TV on request). Excellent
restaurant with mid-week
specials: 3 courses for
£9.95, also bar meals.
Friendly service.**

Guesthouses/B & Bs

Mrs Wood,
Oak Garth Farm,
North End,
Osmotherley,
Northallerton,
N Yorks DL6 3BH
Tel: (0609) 83314
Guide Price: £10.50

Mr & Mrs Gardner,
Hemel Stones,
Clack Lane,
Osmotherley,
Northallerton,
N Yorks DL6 3PP
Tel: (0609) 83313
Guide Price: from £9.50

Mr & Mrs Boyes,
Vane House,
11a North End,
Osmotherley,
Northallerton,
N Yorks DL6 3BA
Tel: (0609) 83448
Guide Price: £11

Mr & Mrs Buck,
Post Office,
Osmotherley,
Northallerton,
N Yorks DL6 3AA
Tel: (0609) 83201
Guide Price: £11

Dr Bainbridge,
Quintana House,
Back Lane,
Osmotherley,
Northallerton,
N Yorks DL6 3BJ
Tel: (0609) 83258
Guide Price: £10

Budget

Hostel (YHA),
Cote Ghyll,
Osmotherley,
Northallerton,
N Yorks DL6 3AH
Tel: (060983) 575
Guide Price: £5.90

CARLTON IN CLEVELAND

The Blackwell Ox,
Carlton-in-Cleveland,
Stokesley,
N Yorks TS9 7DJ
Tel: (0642) 712287
Guide Price: £16

CRINGLE MOOR

B & B and camping,
Mrs Cook,
Beakhills Farm,
Chop Gate,
Middlesborough,
Cleveland TS9 7AR
Tel: (0642) 778368
Guide Price: B & B £10
(camping £1)

GREAT BROUGHTON

Guesthouses/B & Bs

Mrs Sutcliffe,
Ingle Hill,
Ingleby Road,
Great Broughton,
Stokesley,
Cleveland
Tel: (0642) 712449
Guide Price: £12

Mrs Mead,
Hilton House,
52 High Street,
Great Broughton,
Stokesley,
N Yorks TS9 7EG
Tel: (0642) 712526
Guide Price: £12

Mrs Noble,
4, Manor Grove,
Great Broughton,
Stokesley,
N Yorks TS9 7EJ
Tel: (0642) 712291
Guide Price: £12

B & B and camping,
The Swales Family,
White Post Farm,
Great Broughton,
Stokesley,
N Yorks TS9 7HU
Tel: (0642) 778293
Guide Price: B & B £12.50

Mr Robinson,
Holme Farm,
Great Broughton,
Stokesley,
N Yorks TS9 7HF
Tel: (0642) 712345
Guide Price: £10.50

Budget

Campsite,
Toft Hill Farm,
Kirby,
Great Broughton
Middlesborough,
Cleveland TS9 7HJ
Tel: (0642) 712469
Guide Price: £1.50 per person

INGLEBY GREENHOW

Guesthouses/B & Bs

Mrs Swiers,
How Hill Farm,
Ingleby Greenhow,
Great Ayton,
Cleveland TS9 6RD
Tel: (0642) 778288
Guide Price: £10

Mrs Day,
New Sheepfold Farm,
Ingleby Greenhow,
Great Ayton,
Cleveland TS9 6RQ
Tel: (0642) 778393
Guide Price: £12.50

Dr & Mrs Bloom,
Manor House Farm,
Ingleby Greenhow,
Great Ayton,
Cleveland TS9 6RB
Tel: (0642) 722384
Guide Price: from £28.50

BLAKEY

The Lion Inn,
Blakey,
Kirkbymoorside,
N Yorks YO6 6LQ
Tel: (07515) 320
Guide Price: £16.50

B & B,
Mrs Ellerington,
High Blakey House,
Blakey,
North York Moors,
N Yorks YO6 6LQ
Tel: (07515) 641
Guide Price: £15

FARNDALE

Guesthouses/B & Bs

Mrs Stanley,
Head House Farm,
Church House,
Farndale
N Yorks YO6 6LH
Tel: (0751) 33252
Guide Price: £8

Mrs Featherstone,
Keysback Farm,
Farndale,
N Yorks YO6 6UZ
Tel: (0751) 33221
Guide Price: £8.50

Mrs Stanley,
Head House Farm,
Farndale,
N Yorks YO6 6LH
Tel: (0751) 33252
Guide Price: £8

GLAISDALE

Hotels/Inns

**The Arncliffe Arms,
Beggars Bridge,
Glaisdale,
Near Whitby,
N Yorks YO21 2QL
Tel: (0947) 87209
Guide Price: £15
Mike & Angela Westwood.
Dining room, accommodation, bar food, family and function room available.
Coast to Coast walkers and children welcome.**

Anglers Rest Inn,
Glaisdale,
Whitby,
N Yorks YO21 2QH
Tel: (0947) 87261
Guide Price: £16

Mitre Tavern,
Glaisdale,
Whitby,
N Yorks YO21 2PL
Tel: (0947) 87315
Guide Price: £15-£18.50

Guesthouses/B & Bs

**Mrs Langley,
High Gill Beck Farm,
Dalehead,
Glaisdale, Whitby,
N Yorks YO21 2QA
Tel: (0947) 87608**

Sheep graze in the valley of Farndale.

Beggar's Bridge, near Glaisdale: a splendid old packhorse bridge

Guide Price: £10-£12. TV and tea-making facilities in each room. Thermos flasks filled. Shown on Ordnance Survey maps. Peaceful location.

Mrs Macgregor,
Rock Head Farm,
Glaisdale,
Whitby,
N Yorks YO21 2PZ
Tel: (0947) 87355
Guide Price: £11

Mrs Mortimer,
Hollins Farm,
Glaisdale,
Whitby,
N Yorks YO21 2PZ
Tel: (0947) 87516
Guide Price: £9

Egton Banks Farm,
Glaisdale,
Whitby,
N Yorks YO21 2QP
Tel: (0947) 87289
Guide Price: £10

Mrs Spashett,
Red House Farm,
Glaisdale,
Whitby,
N Yorks YO21 2PZ
Tel: (0947) 87242
Guide Price: £12-£18

M R & T Silkstone,
Beggars Bridge Tea Room,
Glaisdale,
Whitby,
N Yorks
Tel: (0947) 87533
Guide Price: from £16.50

Mrs Gullon,
Church Dale Farm,
Glaisdale,
Whitby,
N Yorks YO21 2PZ
Tel: (0947) 87502
Guide Price: £12

Mrs Weighell,
Sycamore Dell,
Glaisdale,
Whitby,
N Yorks YO21 2PZ
Tel: (0947) 87345
Guide Price: £12

EGTON BRIDGE

The Postgate Inn,
Egton Bridge,
Near Whitby,
N Yorks YO21 1UX
Tel: (0947) 85241
Guide Price: £18

GROSMONT

Guesthouses/B & Bs

Janet Bryan,
Woodside,
Front Street,
Grosmont,
N Yorks YO22 5PF
Tel: (0947) 85205
Guide Price: from £11

Mrs Rodgers,
Wood View,
Front Street,
Grosmont,
N Yorks YO22 3AR
Tel: (0947) 85461
Guide Price: £11

Mrs Haslem,
Priory Farm,
Grosmont,
N Yorks YO22 5QQ
Tel: (0947) 85324
Guide Price: £11

Mr Atha,
Hazlewood House,
Front Street,
Grosmont,
N Yorks YO22 5QE
Tel: (0947) 85292
Guide Price: £11

Mrs Hodgson,
Fairhead Farm,
Grosmont,
N Yorks YO22 5TN
Tel: (0947) 85238
Guide Price: from £8

Mrs Prescott,
Grosmont House,
Grosmont,
N Yorks YO22 5PE
Tel: (0947) 85539
Guide Price: £15

HIGH HAWKSER

Guesthouses/B & Bs

Mrs J Walley,
York House Private Hotel,
High Hawkser,
Whitby,
N Yorks YO22 4LW
Tel: (0947) 880314
Guide Price: from £18.40

Mrs Dawson,
The Ridings,
Normanby,
Whitby,
N Yorks YO22 4PF
Tel: (0947) 880451
Guide Price: £15

ROBIN HOODS BAY

Hotels/Inns

Grosvenor Hotel,
Station Road,
Robin Hoods Bay,
Whitby,
N Yorks YO22 4RA
Tel: (0947) 880320
Guide Price: £15

Victoria Hotel,
Robin Hoods Bay,
Whitby,
N Yorks YO22 4RL
Tel: (0947) 880205
Guide Price: £14

Guesthouses/B & Bs

Birtley House Guest House,
Station Road,
Robin Hoods Bay,
N Yorks YO22 6RL
Tel: (0947) 880566
Guide Price: £12

Mr & Mrs Leaf,
Muir Lea Stores,
New Road,
Robin Hoods Bay,
N Yorks YO22 4SF
Tel: (0947) 880316
Guide Price: £10-£12

Mrs Eatough,
Moor View Guest House,
Robin Hoods Bay,
N Yorks YO22 4RA
Tel: (0947) 880576
Guide Price: from £12.50

Mr & Mrs Scrivener,
Plantation House,
Thorpe Lane,
Robin Hoods Bay,
N Yorks
Tel: (0947) 880036
Guide Price: £15

Mrs Timmins,
West Royd Guest House,
Station Road,
Robin Hoods Bay,
Whitby,
N Yorks YO22 4RL
Tel: (0947) 880678
Guide Price: £12

Mrs Luker,
Meadowfield,
Mount Pleasant North,
Robin Hoods Bay,
Whitby,
N Yorks
Tel: (0947) 880564
Guide Price: £13

End of the trail: the steep and narrow streets of Robin Hood's Bay are a welcome sight for Coast to Coast walkers.

Mrs Noble,
Mingo Cottage,
Fylingthorpe,
Robin Hoods Bay,
Whitby,
N Yorks
Tel: (0947) 880219
Guide Price: £11-£12

Mrs Paxton,
Streonshalh,
Mount Pleasant South,
Robin Hoods Bay,
Whitby,
N Yorks
Tel: (0947) 880619
Guide Price: from £12

Mrs Stubbs,
Rosegarth,
Thorpe Lane,
Robin Hoods Bay,
Whitby,
N Yorks YO22 4RN
Tel: (0947) 880578
Guide Price: £12

Budget

Campsite,
Mrs Halder,
Hooks House Farm,
Robin Hoods Bay,
N Yorks YO22 4PE
Tel: (0947) 880283
Guide Price: £1-£1.50 per person

CLEVELAND WAY

The Cleveland Way is a 108-mile walk, inaugurated in 1969, just four years after the Pennine Way. It lies mainly within the North York Moors National Park, offering splendid moorland scenery, extensive views and then, by contrast, a cliff-top walk along the Heritage Coast of Cleveland and North Yorkshire.

The route begins near the market town of Helmsley, and heads west towards the viewpoint of Sutton Bank and the famous white horse at Kilburn, "carved" into a hillside. From here walkers strike north, across the Hambleton and Cleveland Hills, to the equally well-known landmark of Roseberry Topping.

The sea is reached at Saltburn; from here the walk follows the sea-cliffs southwards, taking in some of the finest coastal scenery in the north of England. The dramatic sea views are punctuated by delightful villages such as Staithes and Robin Hoods Bay which, despite their popularity with visitors, still remain authentic fishing villages.

Walkers can explore the harbour at Whitby, and climb the steps to admire the town's famous abbey on the adjacent cliff-top. Scarborough is an altogether busier spot, reflecting its status as Yorkshire's premier seaside resort. The official end of the Cleveland Way is just a few miles further on, at the headland of Filey Brigg.

The Cleveland Way is officially designated as a National Trail, and the route is well waymarked. Walkers will soon become familiar with the Cleveland Way logo — an acorn — which can be found at most junctions and elsewhere as reassurance that they are on the right track. Nevertheless, they should arm themselves with a guidebook to the route (see appendix), and the appropriate maps: OS Outdoor Leisure series, sheets 26 and 27.

The public transport system is not extensive along the Cleveland Way, though there are railway stations on or near the route at Thirsk, Kildale, Great Ayton, Saltburn, Whitby, Scarborough and Filey. Detailed information about bus services are to be found in "Moors Connections" — a booklet available from TICs or from the North York Moors National Park, The Old Vicarage, Bondgate, Helmsley, York YO6 5BP, tel: (0439) 70657.

Also available from this address are a brochure about the Cleveland Way and an accompanying guide to accommodation along the route. Further addresses are featured in the National Park's Visitor Guide.

Suggested daily destinations are Kilburn, Osmotherley, Clay Bank Top, Roseberry Topping, Saltburn, Runswick, Robin Hoods Bay, Scarborough and Filey.

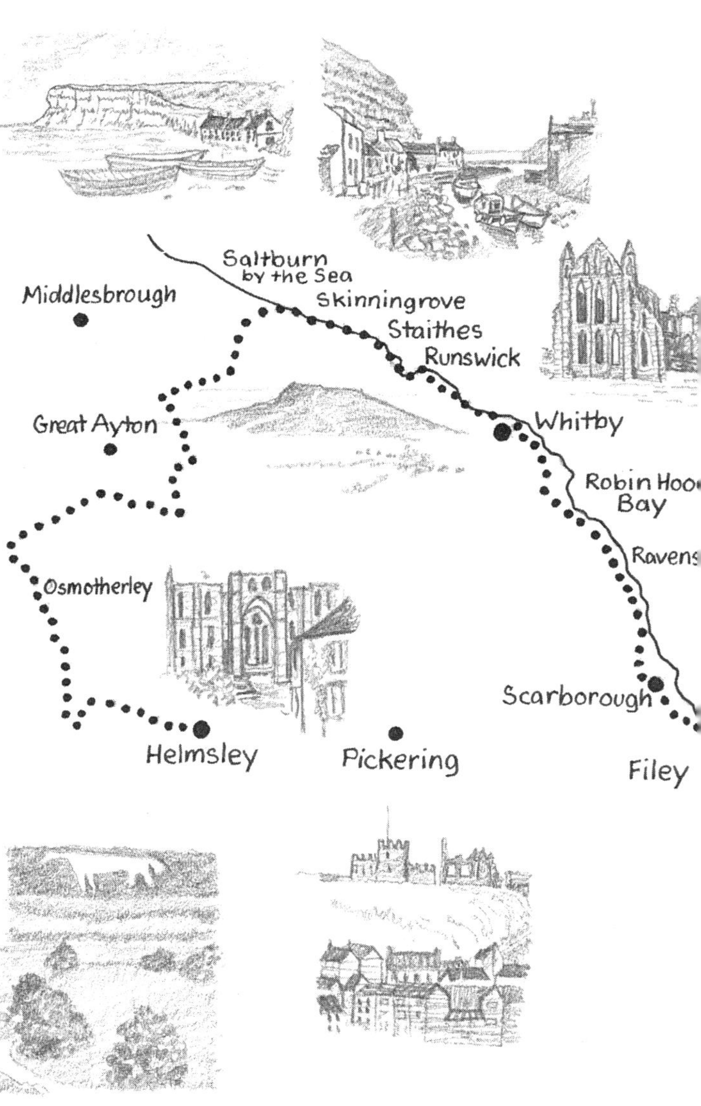
Saltburn
by the Sea
Middlesbrough
Skinningrove
Staithes
Runswick
Great Ayton
Whitby
Robin Hoo
Bay
Ravens
Osmotherley
Scarborough
Helmsley
Pickering
Filey

HELMSLEY

Hotels/Inns

The Crown Hotel,
Market Square,
Helmsley,
N Yorks YO6 5BJ
Tel: (0439) 70297
Guide Price: £24-£26

The Feathers Hotel,
Market Place,
Helmsley,
N Yorks YO6 5BH
Tel: (0439) 70275
Guide Price: £26.50

Mrs Cushworth,
Carlton Lodge Hotel,
53 Bondgate,
Helmsley,
N Yorks
Tel: (0439) 70557
Guide Price: £25

Guesthouses/B & Bs

Mrs Barton,
4 Ashdale Road,
Helmsley,
N Yorks YO6 5DD
Tel: (0439) 70375
Guide Price: £10

Beaconsfield Guest House,
Bondgate,
Helmsley,
N Yorks YO6 5BW
Tel: (0439) 71346
Guide Price: £21-£25

Mrs Easton,
Lockton House,
Bilsdale,
Helmsley,
N Yorks YO6 5NE
Tel: (04396) 303
Guide Price: £11

Mrs Holding,
14 Elmslac Road,
Helmsley,
N Yorks YO6 5AP
Tel: (0439) 70287
Guide Price: £9

Mrs Pooleman,
The Forge,
Hawnby,
Helmsley,
N Yorks
Tel: (04396) 371
Guide Price: £11

Mrs Wood,
Buckingham House,
33 Bridge Street,
Helmsley,
N Yorks YO6 5DX
Tel: (0439) 70613
Guide Price: £12

Budget

Hostel (YHA),
Carlton Lane,
Helmsley,
N Yorks YO6 5HB
Tel: (0439) 70433
Guide Price: £5.90

Campsite,
Mrs Armstrong,
Golden Square,
Caravan Park & campsite,
Oswaldkirk,
Nr Helmsley,
N Yorks
Tel: (04393) 269
Guide Price: £4.85-£6.65

RIEVAULX

Guesthouses/B & Bs

Mrs Hawkins,
Oscar Park Farm,
Rievaulx,

Helmsley,
N Yorks YO6 5LX
Tel: (04396) 231
Guide Price: £12

Mrs Skilbeck,
Middle Heads Farm,
Rievaulx,
Helmsley,
N Yorks YO6 5LU
Tel: (04396) 251
Guide Price: £12

OLD BYLAND

B & B,
Mrs Robinson,
Valley View Farm,
Old Byland,
Helmsley,
N Yorks
Tel: (04396) 221
Guide Price: £18

SUTTON BANK

Guesthouses/B & Bs

Mrs Hope,
High House Farm,
Sutton Bank,
Thirsk,
N Yorks YO7 2HA
Tel: (0845) 597557
Guide Price: £11

Mrs Jeffray,
Hambleton Cottages,
Sutton Bank,
Thirsk,
N Yorks
Tel: (0845) 597363
Guide Price: £11

Mrs Lewis,
Hambleton Lodge,
Thirsk,
N Yorks YO7 2HA
Tel: (0845) 597288
Guide Price: £14

CARLTON HUSTHWAITE

B & B,
Mrs Price,
Carlton Hall,
Carlton Husthwaite,
Thirsk,
N Yorks YO7 2BR
Tel: (0845) 401272
Guide Price: £13-£15

THIRLBY

B & B,
Mrs Stevens,
Skipton Hill Farm,
Thirlby,
Thirsk,
N Yorks YO7 2DQ
Tel: (0845) 597286
Guide Price:

OLDSTEAD

The Black Swan Inn,
Oldstead,
Coxwold,
N Yorks YO6 4BL
Tel: (03476) 387
Guide Price: £19.50

KILBURN

Guesthouses/B & Bs

Mrs Thompson,
Church Farm,
Kilburn,
N Yorks YO6 4AH
Tel: (03476) 318
Guide Price: £12

Mrs Thompson,
Village Farm,
Kilburn,
N Yorks YO6 4AG
Tel: (03476) 562
Guide Price: £12.50

BOLTBY

Guesthouses/B & Bs

**B & B & camping,
Mrs Stephenson,
High Paradise Farm,
Boltby,
Thirsk,
N Yorks YO7 2HT
Tel: (0845) 537353
Guide Price: £12-£15.
On the Cleveland Way, a day's walk from Helmsley. Comfortable old farmhouse; sitting room with TV, full central heating (and log fires). Evening meals, packed lunches and overnight camping.**

Hesketh Hall,
Boltby,
Thirsk,
N Yorks YO7 2HU,
Tel: (0845) 537359
Guide Price: £14-£15

Budget

Campsite,
Mrs Stephenson,
High Paradise Farm,
Boltby,
Thirsk,
N Yorks YO7 2HT
Tel: (0845) 537353
Guide Price: £1 per person

OSMOTHERLEY

**Queen Catherine Hotel,
7 West End,
Osmotherley,
Northallerton,
N Yorks DL6 3AG
Tel: (0609) 83209
Family-run pub/hotel,**

The Yorkshire uplands, unfit for arable farming, provide good grazing for sheep.

Osmotherley, with its striking market cross, is one of the first ports of call for Cleveland Way walkers.

£16.50 with full breakfast. Rooms warm & comfortable with tea & coffee facilities (TV on request). Excellent restaurant with mid-week specials: 3 courses for £9.95, also bar meals. Friendly service.

Guesthouses/B & Bs

Mr & Mrs Buck,
Post Office,
Osmotherley,
Northallerton,
N Yorks DL6 3AA
Tel: (0609) 83201
Guide Price: £11

Mrs Wood,
Oak Garth Farm,
North End,
Osmotherley,
Northallerton,
N Yorks DL6 3BH
Tel: (0609) 83314
Guide Price: £10.50

Mr & Mrs Gardner,
Hemel Stones,
Clack Lane,
Osmotherley,
Northallerton,
N Yorks DL6 3PP
Tel: (0609) 83313
Guide Price: from £9.50

Mr & Mrs Boyes,
Vane House,
11a North End,
Osmotherley,
Northallerton,
N Yorks DL6 3BA
Tel: (0609) 83448
Guide Price: £11

Dr Bainbridge,
Quintana House,
Back Lane,
Osmotherley,
Northallerton DL6 3BJ
Tel: (0609) 83258
Guide Price: £10

Budget

Hostel (YHA),
Cote Ghyll,
Osmotherley,
Northallerton,
N Yorks DL6 3AH
Tel: (060983) 575
Guide Price: £5.90

INGLEBY CROSS

B & B,
Mrs Hillary,
Ox-hill Farm,
Ingleby Cross,
Northallerton DL6 3NJ
Tel: (0609) 82255
Guide Price: £11

B & B and campsite,
North York Moors Adventure Centre,
Park House,
Ingleby Cross,
Near Osmotherley,
Northallerton DL6 3PE
Tel: (0609) 82571
Guide Price: B & B £10,
camping 50p per person

CRINGLE MOOR

B & B and campsite,
Mrs Cook,
Beakhills Farm,
Chopgate,
Stokesley,
N Yorks TS9 7JJ
Tel: (0642) 778368
Guide Price: £10

GREAT BROUGHTON

Guesthouses/B & Bs

Mrs Sutcliffe,
Ingle Hill,
Ingleby Road,
Great Broughton,
Stokesley,
Cleveland
Tel: (0642) 712449
Guide Price: £12

Mrs Mead,
Hilton House,
52 High Street,
Great Broughton,
Stokesley,
N Yorks TS9 7EG
Tel: (0642) 712526
Guide Price: £12

Mrs Noble,
4 Manor Grove,
Great Broughton,
Stokesley,
N Yorks TS9 7EJ
Tel: (0642) 712291
Guide Price: £12

B & B and camping,
The Swales Family,
White Post Farm,
Great Broughton,
Stokesley,
N Yorks TS9 7HU
Tel: (0642) 778293
Guide Price: B & B £12.50

Mr Robinson,
Holme Farm,
Great Broughton,
Stokesley,
N Yorks TS9 7HF
Tel: (0642) 712345
Guide Price: £10.50

Budget

Campsite,
Toft Hill Farm,
Kirby,
Great Broughton,
Middlesborough,
Cleveland TS9 7HJ
Tel: (0642) 712469
Guide Price: £1.50 per person

INGLEBY GREENHOW

Guesthouses/B & Bs

Dr & Mrs Bloom,
Manor House Farm,
Ingleby Greenhow,
Great Ayton,
N Yorks TS9 6RB
Tel: (0642) 722384
Guide Price: from £17.50

Mrs Day,
New Sheepfold Farm,
Ingleby Greenhow,
Great Ayton,
N Yorks TS9 6RQ
Tel: (0642) 778393
Guide Price: £12.50

KILDALE

Guesthouses/B & Bs

Mrs Addison,
Bankside Cottage,
Kildale,
Whitby,
Cleveland YO21 2RT
Tel: (0642) 723259
Guide Price: £12

Mrs Howard,
Oak Tree Farm,
Lonsdale,
Kildale,
Whitby,
Cleveland YO21 2RU
Tel: (0642) 722511
Guide Price: £12

GUISBOROUGH

Hotels/Inns

Three Fiddles Hotel,
Westgate,
Guisborough,
Cleveland TS14 6ND
Tel: (0287) 632417
Guide Price: £20

Fox and Hounds Hotel,
Slapewath,
Guisborough,
Cleveland TS14 6PX
Tel: (0287) 632964
Guide Price: £27

Moorcock Hotel,
West End Road,
Guisborough,
Cleveland TS14 6RL
Tel: (0287) 632342
Guide Price: £18-£25

Guesthouses/B & Bs

Mrs Waller,
200 Enfield Chase,
Guisborough,
Cleveland TS14 7LG
Tel: (0287) 633687
Guide Price: £11

Budget

Campsite,
Mr & Mrs Wainwright,
Tocketts Mill Caravan Park,
Skelton Road,
Guisborough,
Cleveland TS14 6QA
Tel: (0287) 610182
Guide Price: £6-£7

SKELTON

B & B,
Mr & Mrs Bull,
Westerlands Guest House,
27 East Parade,
Skelton,
Saltburn-by-Sea,
Cleveland TS12 2BJ
Tel: (0287) 50690
Guide Price: £11-£16

SALTBURN-by-SEA

Hotels/Inns

Mrs Noble,
Crake Hall Hotel,
79 Marine Parade,
Saltburn-by-Sea,
Cleveland TS12 1EL
Tel: (0287) 623839
Guide Price: £18

The village of Great Ayton has many historical associations with Captain Cook.

Staithes has kept the character of a traditional fishing village, despite the influx of visitors.

Cliffedene Hotel,
50, Ruby Street,
Saltburn-by-Sea,
Cleveland TS12 1EG
Tel: (0287) 622367
Guide Price: £11

Guesthouses/B & Bs

Mr Blueitt,
Rockville,
31 Diamond Street,
Saltburn-by-Sea,
Cleveland TS12 1EB,
Tel: (0287) 624074
Guide Price: £10

Mrs Malbon,
Avimore Hall,
27 Pearl Street,
Saltburn-by-Sea,
Cleveland TS12 1DU
Tel: (0287) 624664
Guide Price: £12.50

Albany Guest House,
15 Pearl Street,
Saltburn-by-Sea,
Cleveland TS12 1DU
Tel: (0287) 622221
Guide Price: £10.50-£12

Mrs Priestley,
Treharne,
46 Garnet Street,
Saltburn-by-Sea,
Cleveland TS12 1EN
Tel: (0287) 622193
Guide Price: £12.50

Blue Rose Guest House,
34, Emerald Street,
Saltburn-by-Sea,
Cleveland TS12 1ED
Tel: (0287) 623864
Guide Price: £12.50

Mrs Game,
Briars Guest House,
24 Pearl Street,
Saltburn-by-Sea,
Cleveland TS12 1DU
Tel: (0287) 622264
Guide Price: £11.50-£21

Mrs Stage,
Rackmans,
34 Pearl Street,
Saltburn-by-Sea,
Cleveland TS12 1DU
Tel: (0287) 623905
Guide Price: £11.50-£14.50

Budget

Campsite,
Margrove Park Holidays,
Boosbeck,
Saltburn-by-Sea,
Cleveland TS12 3BZ
Tel: (0287) 53616
Guide Price: £2.50-£3.50 per person

Campsite,
"Serenity"
Hinderwell,
Saltburn-by-Sea,
Cleveland TS13 5JH
Tel: (0947) 6840523
Guide Price:

Hostel (YHA),
Riftswood Hall,
Victoria Road,
Saltburn-by-Sea,
Cleveland TS12 1JD
Tel: (0287) 24389
Guide Price: £3.40-£5.50

STAITHES

Hawthorn Grove Hotel,
High Street,
Staithes,
Saltburn-by-Sea,
Cleveland TS13 5BQ
Tel: (0947) 841439
Guide Price: £16

Guesthouses/B & Bs

Mrs Clemmitt,
Borrowby Farm,
Borrowby,
Staithes,
Saltburn-by-Sea,
Cleveland TS13 5EH
Tel: (0947) 840441
Guide Price: £11

Ms Yeomans,
The Old Stables,
Boulby,
Nr Saltburn-by-Sea,
Cleveland TS13 4UR
Tel: (0287) 41109
Guide Price: £10-£16

Endeavour Restaurant,
1 High Street,
Staithes,
Saltburn-by-Sea,
Cleveland
Tel: (0947) 840825
Guide Price: £15-£20

Harbourside Guest House,
Seaton Garth,
Staithes,
Saltburn-by-Sea,
Cleveland
Tel: (0947) 841296
Guide Price: £15-£17.50

PORT MULGRAVE

The Ship Inn,
Port Mulgrave,
Hinderwell,
Saltburn-by-Sea,
Cleveland TS13 5JZ
Tel: (0947) 840303
Guide Price: £13.50

RUNSWICK BAY

The Ellerby Hotel,
Hinderwell,
Saltburn-by-Sea,
Cleveland TS13 5LP
Tel: (0947) 840342
Guide Price: £28

Guesthouses/B & Bs

Mrs Pearson,
Seadale,
Bank Top,
Runswick Bay,
Saltburn-by-Sea,
Cleveland TS13 5HR
Tel: (0947) 840440
Guide Price: £11.60

Mrs Shackleton,
The Firs,
Runswick Bay,
Saltburn-by-Sea,
Cleveland TS13 5HR
Tel: (0947) 840433
Guide Price: £16

SANDSEND

B & B,
Mrs Hodgkinson,
36 Meadowfields,
Sandsend,
Whitby,
N Yorks
Tel: (0947) 83415
Guide Price: £10.50

SLEIGHTS

Salmon Leap Hotel,
Coach Road,
Sleights,
Whitby,
N Yorks YO22 5AA
Tel: (0947) 810233
Guide Price: £15

Guesthouses/B & Bs

Ryedale House,
156 Coach Road,
Sleights, Whitby,
N Yorks YO22 5EQ
Tel: (0947) 810534
Guide Price: £13.50

Mrs Potts,
Willow Dale,
17 Carr Hill Lane,
Sleights,
Whitby,
N Yorks YO21 1RS
Tel: (0947) 810525
Guide Price: £14-20

WHITBY

Hotels/Inns

Kimberley Hotel,
7 Havelock Place,
Whitby,
N Yorks YO21 3ER
Tel: (0947) 604125
Guide Price: £20-£28

Mrs Thompson,
Arundel House,
Bagdale,
Whitby,
N Yorks YO21 1QJ
Tel: (0947) 603645
Guide Price: £15-£20

Hotel Carlill,
Royal Crescent,
Westcliff,
Whitby,
N Yorks
Tel: (0947) 602349
Guide Price: £10-£12

Guesthouses/B & Bs

Mrs Hall,
The Old Mill,
Littlebeck,
Whitby,
N Yorks YO22 5HA
Tel: (0947) 810442
Guide Price: £12-£15

Typical sights in Whitby: lobster pots, harbour-side cottages and the ever-present seagulls.

Leeway Guest House,
1 Havelock Place,
Whitby,
N Yorks YO21 3ER
Tel: (0947) 602604
Guide Price: £10-£13

Wentworth Guest House,
27 Hudson Street,
Whitby,
N Yorks YO21 3EP
Tel: (0947) 602433
Guide Price: from £11

Mr & Mrs Collett,
Ashford,
8 Royal Crescent,
Whitby,
N Yorks YO21 3EJ
Tel: (0947) 602138
Guide Price: £12

Falcon Guest House,
29 Falcon Terrace,
Whitby,
N Yorks
Tel: (0947) 603507
Guide Price: £9.50

Mrs Marr,
Heatherlea,
5, Ocean Road,
Whitby,
N Yorks
Tel: (0947) 600980
Guide Price: £10

Mr Robinson,
Larpool Hall,
Whitby,
N Yorks YO22 4ND
Tel: (0947) 602737
Guide Price: £28.50

Mrs Smith,
Haven Guest House,
4, East Crescent,
Whitby,
N Yorks YO21 3DH
Tel: (0947) 603842
Guide Price: £13-£17

Budget

Hostel (YHA),
East Cliff,
Whitby,
N Yorks YO22 4JT
Tel: (0947) 602878
Guide Price: £5.50

Hostel (YHA),
Westerdale,
Whitby,
N Yorks YO21 2DU
Tel: (0287) 60469
Guide Price: £3.20

Campsite,
Northcliffe Holiday Park,
High Hawkser,
Near Whitby,
N Yorks YO22 4LL
Tel: (0947) 880477
Guide Price: from £2 per person to £5 per family tent

Campsite,
Mr Butterfield,
Grouse Hill Caravan Park,
Fylingdales, Whitby,
N Yorks YO22 4QH
Guide Price: from £2 per person to £6 per family tent

ROBIN HOODS BAY

Hotels/Inns

Grosvenor Hotel,
Station Road,
Robin Hoods Bay,
Whitby,
N Yorks YO22 4RA
Tel: (0947) 880320
Guide Price: £15

The houses of Robin Hoods Bay cling precariously to the steep cliffside; it's a place for walkers, not cars.

Victoria Hotel,
Robin Hoods Bay,
Whitby,
N Yorks YO22 4RL
Tel: (0947) 880205
Guide Price: £14

Guesthouses/B & Bs

Birtley House Guest House,
Station Road,
Robin Hoods Bay,
Whitby,
N Yorks YO22 6RL
Tel: (0947) 880566
Guide Price: £12

Mr & Mrs Leaf,
Muir Lea Stores,
New Road,
Robin Hoods Bay,
Whitby,
N Yorks YO22 4SF
Tel: (0947) 880316
Guide Price: £10-£12

Mrs Eatough,
Moor View Guest House,
Robin Hoods Bay,
Whitby,
N Yorks YO22 4RA
Tel: (0947) 880576
Guide Price: from £12.50

Mr & Mrs Scrivener,
Plantation House,
Thorpe Lane,
Robin Hoods Bay,
Whitby,
N Yorks
Tel: (0947) 880036
Guide Price: £15

Mrs Luker,
Meadowfield,
Mount Pleasant North,
Robin Hoods Bay,
Whitby,
N Yorks
Tel: (0947) 880564
Guide Price: £13

Mrs Noble,
Mingo Cottage,
Fylingthorpe,
Robin Hoods Bay,
Whitby,
N Yorks
Tel: (0947) 880219
Guide Price: £11-£12

Mrs Paxton,
Streonshalh,
Mount Pleasant South,
Robin Hoods Bay,
Whitby,
N Yorks
Tel: (0947) 880619
Guide Price: from £12

Mrs Stubbs,
Rosegarth,
Thorpe Lane,
Robin Hoods Bay,
Whitby,
N Yorks YO22 4RN
Tel: (0947) 880578
Guide Price: £12

Mrs Timmins,
West Royd Guest House,
Station Road,
Robin Hoods Bay,
Whitby
N Yorks YO22 4RL
Tel: (0947) 880678
Guide Price: £12

Budget

Campsite,
Mrs Halder,
Hooks House Farm,
Robin Hoods Bay,
Whitby,
N Yorks YO22 4PE
Tel: (0947) 880283
Guide Price: £1-£1.50 per person

Hostel (YHA),
Boggle Hole,
Mill Beck,
Fylingthorpe,
Whitby,
N Yorks YO22 4UG
Tel: (0947) 880352
Guide Price: £6.30

RAVENSCAR

Guesthouses/B & B

Mrs Pease,
Ness Hall,
Ravenscar,
Scarborough,
N Yorks YO13 0LX
Tel: (0723) 870536
Guide Price: from £11.50

Mrs Pilley,
Crag Hill,
Ravenhill Road,
Ravenscar,
Scarborough, N Yorks
Tel: (0723) 870925
Guide Price: £14-£16

B & B & campsite,
Mrs White,
Bent Rigg Farm,
Ravenscar,
Scarborough, N Yorks
Tel: (0723) 870475
Guide Price: B & B £8.50

Mrs Greenfield,
Smugglers Rock,
Country Guest House,
Ravenscar,
Scarborough,
N Yorks YO13 OER
Tel: (0723) 870044
Guide Price: £15.50

Mrs Leach,
Bide-a-While,
3 Lorings Road,
Ravenscar,
Scarborough,
N Yorks YO13 0LY
Tel: (0723) 870643
Guide Price: £10

STAINTONDALE

The Shepherd's Arms,
Staintondale,
Scarborough,
N Yorks
Tel: (0723) 870257
Guide Price: £13

**B & B and campsite,
Lowfields,
Downdale Road,
Staintondale,
Scarborough,
N Yorks YO13 0EZ
Tel: (0723) 870574
Seven miles north of Scarborough, close to Cleveland Way & Lyke Wake Walk. Shower/toilet block; basic foods available for campers. Static caravans for hire.**

B & B
Mrs Edmondson,
Plane Tree Cottage Farm,
Staintondale,
Scarborough,
N Yorks YO13 OEY
Tel: (0723) 870796
Guide Price: £12

CLOUGHTON

B & B,
Mrs Marton,
Gowland Farm,
Gowland Lane,
Cloughton,
Scarborough,
N Yorks YO12 0DU
Tel: (0723) 870924
Guide Price: £10

SCALBY

Campsite,
Mrs Thompson,
Beacon Cottage Farm,
Barmoor Lane,
Scalby,
Scarborough,
N Yorks YO13 0PQ
Tel: (0723) 870378
Guide Price: 50p per person

SCARBOROUGH

Hotels/Inns

Green Gables Hotel,
West Bank,
Scarborough,
N Yorks YO12 4DX
Tel: (0723) 361005'
Guide Price: £13

Highbank Hotel,
5 Givendale Road,
Scarborough,
N Yorks YO12 6LE
Tel: (0723) 365265
Guide Price: £10-£11

Ashburton Hotel,
43 Valley Road,
Scarborough,
N Yorks YO11 2LX
Tel: (0723) 374382
Guide Price: £12.50-£13.50

Guesthouses/B & Bs

Cerise Guest House,
2 Elders Street,
Scarborough,
N Yorks YO11 1DZ
Tel: (0723) 360041
Guide Price: £10-£11

Invergarry,
4 St Martins Square,
South Cliff,
Scarborough,
N Yorks YO11 2DQ
Tel: (0723) 372013
Guide Price: from £10

Amber Lodge,
17 Trinity Rolad,
Scarborough,
N Yorks YO11 2TD
Tel: (0723) 369088
Guide Price: £12.50-£14.50

Budget

Hostel (YHA),
The White House,
Burniston Road,
Scarborough,
N Yorks YO13 0DA
Tel: (0723) 361176
Guide Price: £5.50

DALES WAY

The Dales Way, inaugurated in 1968, is less strenuous than the other long-distance walks in this book. It follows rivers — particularly the Wharfe and the Dee — through some of the most beautiful valleys in the North, keeping largely to the lower ground. It is thus suitable for family groups and less experienced walkers, who may want to try it before tackling tougher propositions such as the Pennine Way or Coast to Coast Walk.

The 75 miles of the Dales Way can be walked continuously, or each stage can be regarded as a pleasant day's ramble. The riverside route also means that walkers are never too far away from a hot meal, refreshment and a bed for the night.

The "official" starting point of the Dales Way is Ilkley, a stately old spa town, though there are interesting link paths for walkers stepping out from Leeds and Bradford. Walkers from Leeds can enjoy a surprisingly rural route almost from the city centre.

Walkers are guided up the valley of the Wharfe, taking in pleasant villages such as Grassington and Kettlewell. From Langstrothdale the route follows the River Dee, through the lush valley of Dentdale, and accompanies the rivers Rawthey, Lune and Kent to the final destination of Bowness, on the shores of Lake Windermere.

The rivers themselves — and the wildlife they support — are perhaps the major attraction of the Dales Way. Other bonuses are the easy walking, ever-changing views, splendid old bridges and riverside pubs. Among other features to be seen along the way are prehistoric sites, ancient packhorse tracks and the many little Dales villages of sturdy, stone-built cottages.

The route can be conveniently split into the following sections, with each day's mileage in brackets. But the ready availability of accommodation makes other options possible.

Ilkley to Barden (12)
Barden to Grassington (7)
Grassington to Buckden (12)
Buckden to Dentdale (16)
Dentdale to Sedbergh (11)
Sedbergh to Burneside (15)
Burneside to Bowness (8)

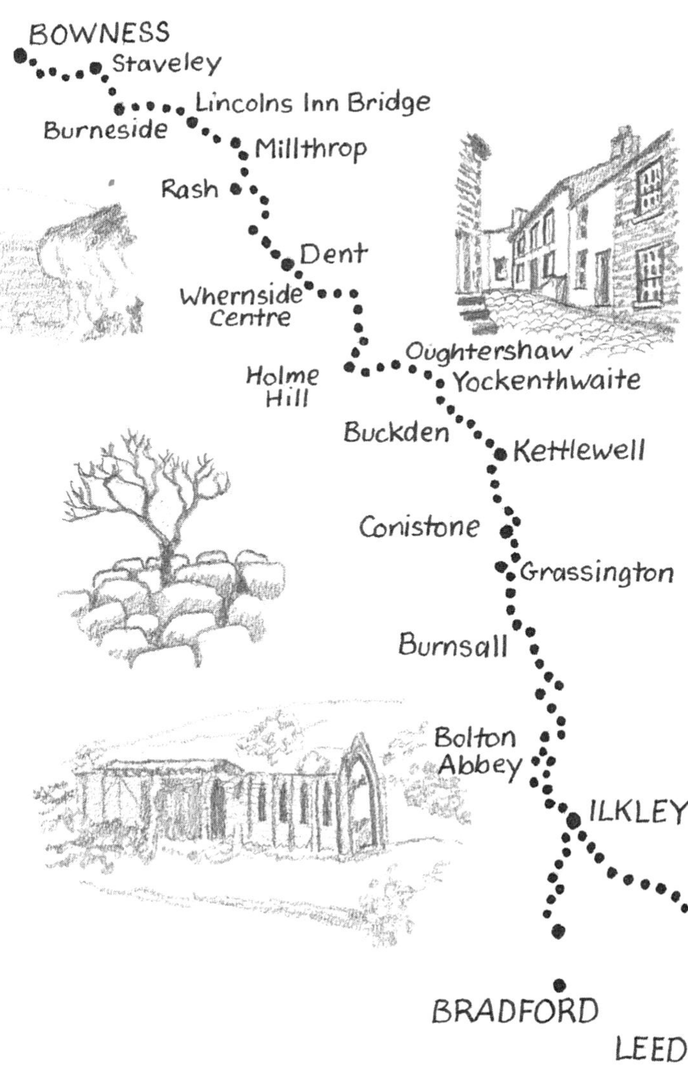
BOWNESS
Staveley
Lincolns Inn Bridge
Burneside
Millthrop
Rash
Dent
Whernside Centre
Oughtershaw
Holme Hill
Yockenthwaite
Buckden
Kettlewell
Conistone
Grassington
Burnsall
Bolton Abbey
ILKLEY
BRADFORD
LEED.

OTLEY

Guesthouses/B & Bs

Riverdale Guest House,
1 Riverdale Road,
Otley,
W Yorks
Tel: (0943) 461387
Guide Price: £16-£20

Tormore Guest House,
55 Boroughgate,
Otley,
W Yorks
Tel: (0943) 465852
Guide Price: £13-£15

ILKLEY

Hotels/Inns

Rose & Crown,
Church Street,
Ilkley,
West Yorks
Tel: (0943) 607260
Guide Price: £20-£30

Guesthouses/B & Bs

Mrs Battey,
Belmost,
Queens Road,
Ilkley,
West Yorks
Tel: (0943) 602445
Guide Price: £15-£28

Mr & Mrs Witherington,
Glengarth,
3 Grange Estate,
off Valley Drive,
Ilkley,
Tel: (0943) 607260
Guide Price: £20-£30

Mrs C Minto,
Briarwood,
Queens Drive
Ilkley,
West Yorks
Tel: (0943) 600870
Guide Price: £12-£14

Mrs Whitehead,
3 Victoria Gardens,

The River Wharfe at Otley.

Bolton Abbey occupies a splendid site, in a crook of the River Wharfe.

Ilkley,
West Yorks
Tel: (0943) 607891
Guide Price: £12.50

Mrs Below,
Archway Cottage,
24 Skipton Road,
Ilkley,
West Yorks
Tel: (0943) 603399
Guide Price: £13.50-£17

Mrs Y O'Neill,
Poplar View Guest House,
8 Bolton Bridge Road,
Ilkley,
W Yorks LS29 9AA
Tel: (0943) 608436
Guide Price: £13

Hollygarth House,
293 Leeds Road,
Ilkley,
West Yorks
Tel: (0943) 609223
Guide Price: £12

Mr & Mrs Voss,
Summerhill Guesthouse,
24 Crossbeck Road,
Ilkley,
W Yorks LS29 9JN
Tel: (0943) 607067
Guide Price: £12

Mrs Kemp,
Daleside,
12 Manley Road,
Ilkley,
W Yorks
Tel: (0943) 602962
Guide Price: £9.50

Mrs Kirkland,
Lauridor,
236 Leeds Road,
Ilkley,
W Yorks
Tel: (0943) 607809
Guide Price: £10-£10.50

Mrs Terry,
Belvedere,
2 Victoria Avenue,
Ilkley,
W Yorks
Tel: (0943) 607598
Guide Price: £9.

Mrs Read,
126 Skipton Road,
Ilkley,
W Yorks
Tel: (0943) 600635
Guide Price: £15

Mrs Fidler,
Beech House,
5 St James Road,
Ilkley,
W Yorks
Tel: (0943) 601995
Guide Price: £11-£15

Mrs Coleman,
6 Woodlands Rise,
Grove Park,
Ilkley,
W Yorks
Tel: (0943) 608889
Guide Price: £9

Mrs Bradbury,
1 Tivoli Place,
Ilkley,
W Yorks
Tel: (0943) 609483
Guide Price: £11.50-£13

Moorview Guest House,
104 Skipton Road,
Ilkley,
W Yorks
Tel: (0943) 600156
Guide Price : £16-£22

ADDINGHAM

Guesthouses/B & Bs

Mrs Wilkinson,
Olicana Cottage,
High Mill Lane,
Addingham,
W Yorks
Tel: (0943) 830500
Guide Price: £12

Mrs Goodwin,
27 Wharfe Park,
Addingham,
W Yorks
Tel: (0943) 831370
Guide Price: £10

Mrs Hughes,
176 Main Street,
Addingham,
W Yorks
Tel: (0943) 830038
Guide Price: £9.50-£10

Walls and barns: a typical scene in the Yorkshire Dales.

BOLTON ABBEY

B & B,
Mrs Crabtree,
Bolton Park Farm,
Bolton Abbey,
Skipton,
N Yorks BD23 6AW
Tel: (075671) 244
Guide Price: £11

BARDEN

Guesthouses/B & Bs

Mrs Parkinson,
Holme House Farm,
Barden,
Near Burnsall,
Skipton,
N Yorks BD 23 6AT
Tel: (075672) 661
Guide Price: £10-£12

Mrs Banks,
Scale Farm,
Barden,
near Burnsall,
Skipton,
N Yorks BD23 6AP
Tel: (075672) 648

B & B and campsite,
Mrs Foster,
Howgill Lodge,
Barden,
Near Burnsall,
Skipton,
N Yorks BD23 6DJ
Tel: (075672) 655
Guide price: B & B £20-22

Budget

Bunkhouse Barn,
Mr Leak,
High Garmsworth Cottage,
Barden,
Skipton,
N Yorks BD23 6DH
Tel: (075672) 630
Guide Price: £4.50

APPLETREEWICK

The New Inn,
Appletreewick,
Skipton,
N Yorks BD23 6DA
Tel: (075672) 252
Guide Price: £17.50-£19

B & B,
Mrs Baron,
Haughside,
Appletreewick,
Skipton,
N Yorks BD23 6DQ
Tel: (075672) 225
Guide Price: £12-£16

Campsite,
Mr & Mrs Mason,
Mill Lane,
Appletreewick,
Skipton,
N Yorks BD23 6DD
Tel: (075672) 275/236
Guide Price: £1.80 per person

Burnsall

Hotels/Inns

Red Lion Hotel,
Burnsall,
Grassington,
N Yorks
Tel: (075672) 204
Guide Price: £18-£27

Manor House Hotel,
Burnsall,
Skipton,
N Yorks BD23 6BW
Tel: (075672) 231
Guide Price: £20

The Fell Hotel,
Burnsall,
Skipton,
N Yorks
Tel: (075672) 209
Guide Price: £30.50

Guesthouses/B & Bs

Mrs Wallace,
The Green,
Burnsall,
Skipton,
N Yorks BD23 6ABS
Tel: (075672) 210
Guide Price: £12.50

Mr Mason,
Conistone House,
Burnsall,
Skipton,
N Yorks BD23 6BN
Tel: (075672) 650
Guide Price: £15

LINTON

Hostel (YHA),
Linton,
The Old Rectory,
Linton-in-Craven,
Skipton,
N Yorks BD23 5HH
Tel: (0756) 752400
Guide Price: £6.30

GRASSINGTON

Hotels/Inns

Grassington House Hotel,
The Square,
Grassington,
Wharfedale,
N Yorks
Tel: (0756) 752406
Guide Price: £25

A pattern of limestone walls dividing up the lush fields near Grassington.

Foresters Arms

Proprietor — W A Chaney

Main Street
Grassington,
Skipton
North Yorkshire

Bed and breakfast from £15.00

Colour TV lounge
Tea making facilities
Residential
Home cooking
Hot & cold in all rooms

This famous old coaching inn is situated in the heart of Grassington. Ideal centre for walking or touring, within easy reach of York, Harrogate, Leeds, Brontë Country and the Lake District. Sports facilities easily available, including fishing, bowling, swimming, golf, squash, snooker, etc

Foresters Arms,
Grassington,
Skipton,
N Yorks BD23 5AA
Tel: (0756) 752349
Guide Price: £15

Ashfield House Hotel,
Main Street,
Grassington,
N Yorks
Tel: (0756) 752584
Guide Price: £31-£34

Black Horse Hotel,
Garrs Lane,
Grassington,
N Yorks
Tel: (0756) 752770
Guide Price: £27

Guesthouses/B & Bs

Ray & Marian Lister,
Town Head Guest House,
1 Low Lane,
Grassington,
N Yorks BD23 5AU
Tel: (0756) 752811
Guide Price: £13-£16.
Comfortable accommodation, H & C all rooms, colour TVs, tea-making facilities. Fire certificate, ETB 2 crowns commended. Ideal centre for tourism & walking the Dales.

Mr & Mrs Benson,
Raines Close Guesthouse,
Grassington,
Skipton,
N Yorks BD23 5LS
Tel: (0756) 752678
Guide Price: £14-£20

Mr & Mrs Chaney,
New Laithe House,
Wood Lane,
Grassington,
Skipton,
N Yorks BD23 5LU
Tel: (0756) 752764
Guide Price: £15-£18

Mr & Mrs Colley,
Lythe End,
Wood Lane,
Grassington,
Skipton,
N Yorks BD23 5DF
Tel: (0756) 753196
Guide Price: £14

Mrs Cullingford,
Craven Cottage,
Main Street,
Grassington,
Skipton,
N Yorks BD23 5AA
Tel: (0756) 752205
Guide Price: £14.50

Miss Whitehead,
16 Wood Lane,
Grassington,
Skipton,
N Yorks BD23 5LU
Tel: (0756) 752841
Guide Price: £8.50

Mr Lingard,
The Lodge,
8 Wood Lane,
Grassington,
Skipton,
N Yorks BD23 5LU
Tel: (0756) 752518
Guide Price: £15-£19

Mr & Mrs Ramsden,
Craiglands,
Brooklyn,
Grassington,
Skipton,
N Yorks BD23 5ER
Tel: (0756) 752093
Guide Price: £16

Kirkfield,
Hebden Road,
Grassington,
Skipton,
N Yorks BD23 5LJ
Tel: (0756) 752385
Guide Price: £14

Mrs Mann,
Rostellan,
11 Station Road,
Grassington,
Skipton,
N Yorks BD23 5LS
Tel: (0756) 752687
Guide Price: £14

Mr & Mrs Marsden,
Burtree Cottage,
Hebden Road,
Grassington,
Skipton,
N Yorks BD23 5LH
Tel: (0756) 752442
Guide Price: £11.50

Mrs Paling,
Brownfold Cottage,
Grassington,
Skipton,
N Yorks BD23 5AB
Tel: (0756) 752314
Guide Price: £15

Mr & Mrs Roundhill,
Shalom,
17 Low Lane,
Grassington,
Skipton,
N Yorks BD23 5AU
Tel: (0756) 752964
Guide Price: £13

The Dales Way passes this splendid limestone pavement above Conistone Dib.

Mr Whitfield,
No 47 Restaurant,
Main Street,
Grassington,
Skipton,
N Yorks BD23 5BB
Tel: (0756) 752069,
Guide Price: £20

Mrs Berry,
Springroyd House,
8A Station Road,
Grassington,
N Yorks
Tel: (0756) 752473
Guide Price: £12

Greenways Guest House,
Wharfeside Avenue,
Threshfield,
Nr Grassington,
N Yorks
Tel: (0756) 752598
Guide Price: £18

KILNSEY

Tennant Arms Hotel,
Kilnsey,
Wharfedale,
N Yorks BD23 5PS
Tel: (0756) 752301
Guide Price: £27.50

B & B,
Mrs Cawley & Mr Marston,
Chapel House,
Kilnsey,
Skipton,
N Yorks BD23 5PR
Tel: (0756) 752654
Guide Price: £17-£18

Bunkbarn,
Mrs Foster,
Northcote,
Kilnsey,
Skipton,
N Yorks BD23 5PT
Tel: (0756) 752465
Guide Price: £5 (booking essential)

CONISTONE

B & B,
Mrs Roberts,
Mossdale,
Conistone,
Skipton,
N Yorks BD23 5HS
Tel: (0756) 752320
Guide Price: £12

KETTLEWELL

Hotels/Inns

Blue Bell Hotel,
Middle Lane,
Kettlewell,
N Yorks
Tel: (075676) 230
Guide Price: £20-£24

Guesthouses/B & Bs

Langcliffe House,
Kettlewell,
N Yorks
Tel: (075676) 243
Guide Price: from £25

Mr & Mrs Lambert,
Fold Farm,
Kettlewell,
Skipton,
N Yorks BD23 5RJ
Tel: (075676) 886
Guide Price: £15

Dale House Country Guest House,
Kettlewell,
Skipton,
N Yorks
Tel: (075676) 836
Guide Price: £25

Mr & Mrs Proudfoot,
Fern House,
Kettlewell,
Skipton,
N Yorks BD23 5QX
Tel: (075676) 251
Guide Price: £25

Mrs Thornborrow,
Lynburn,
Langcliffe Garth,
Kettlewell,
Skipton,
N Yorks BD23 5RF
Tel: (075676) 803
Guide Price: £15

Budget

Hostel (YHA),
Whernside House,
Kettlewell,
Skipton,
N Yorks BD23 5HS
Tel: (075676) 232
Guide Price: £5.90

The broad valley of Wharfedale, with Kilnsey Crag in the background.

STARBOTTON

Fox and Hounds,
Starbotton,
Skipton,
N Yorks BD23 5HY
Tel: (075676) 269
Guide Price: £20

Guesthouses/B & Bs

**Mrs Close,
Calfhalls Farm,
Starbotton,
Skipton,
N Yorks BD23 5HY
Tel: (075676) 370
Guide Price: £15**

Mr Rathmell,
Hilltop Country Guest House,
Starbotton,
Skipton,
N Yorks BD23 5HY
Tel: (075676) 321
Guide Price: £24

BUCKDEN

The Buck Inn,
Buckden,
Skipton,
N Yorks BD23 5JA
Tel: (075676) 227
Guide Price: £29.25

Guesthouses/B & Bs

Miss Thornborrow,
West Winds Cottage,
Buckden,
Skipton,
N Yorks BD23 5JA
Tel: (075676) 883
Guide Price: £12

Mrs Oxford,
Mullions,
Buckden,
Skipton,
N Yorks BD23 5JA
Tel: (075676) 252
Guide Price: £13

In Langstrothdale the infant River Wharfe rushes over a series of delightful little waterfalls.

Mr & Mrs Leach
Ghyll Cottage,
Buckden,
Skipton,
N Yorks BD23 5JA
Tel: (075676) 340
Guide Price: £13

Mr Horseman,
Ivy Cottage,
Buckden,
Skipton,
N Yorks BD23 5JA
Tel: (075676) 827
Guide Price: £13

HUBBERHOLME

The George Inn,
Hubberholme,
Near Buckden,
Skipton,
N Yorks
Tel: (075676) 223
Guide Price: £17

Guesthouses/B & Bs

Mrs Edwardes,
Kirkgill Manor Guesthouse,
Hubberholme,
Skipton,
N Yorks BD23 5JE
Tel: (075676) 800
Guide Price: £22.50

B & B and bunkbarn,
Mrs Falshaw,
Grange Farm,
Hubberholme,
Skipton,
N Yorks BD23 5JE
Tel: (075676) 259
Guide Price: Bunkbarn £3.50-£4.50, B & B: £12.50-£14.50

Mrs Huck,
Church Farm,
Hubberholme,
Skipton,
N Yorks BD23 5JE
Tel: (075676) 241

LANGSTROTHDALE

Guesthouses/B & Bs

B & B & bunkhouse barn,
Mrs Dorothy Smith,
Cam Houses,
Upper Langstrothdale,
Buckden,
Skipton,
N Yorks BD23 5JT
Tel: (086064) 8045
Guide Price: B & B £12, bunkbarn £4.50 (children £3.50)

Mrs Burrow,
Elm Cottage,
Oughtershaw,
Buckden,
Skipton,
N Yorks BD23 5JR
Tel: (075676) 322
Guide Price: £12.50

Mrs Middleton,
Low Raisgill,
Yockenthwaite,
Skipton,
N Yorks BD23 5JQ
Tel: (075676) 351
Guide Price: £13.50-£15

Budget

Bunkhouse Barn,
Mrs Bentley,
Hazel Bank Farm,
Oughtershaw,
Buckden, Skipton,
N Yorks BD23 5JR
Tel: (075676) 312
Guide Price: £5

DENTDALE

Hotels/Inns

Sportsman's Inn,
Cowgill, Dent,
Sedbergh,
Cumbria LA10 5RG
Tel: (05875) 282
Guide Price: £14.30

Guesthouses/B & Bs

Mrs Hunter,
Rash House,
Dent Foot,
Cumbria LA10 5SU
Tel: (05396) 20113
Guide Price: £11.50

Mrs Parkes,
Carley Hall Cottage,
Cowgill,
Dentdale,
Cumbria LA10 5RL
Tel: (05875) 244
Guide Price: £11.50

The church at Cautley, with the rounded contours of the Howgill hills as a backdrop.

Mrs Ferguson,
Scow Cottage,
Dent Head,
Sedbergh,
Cumbria LA10 5RN
Tel: (05875) 445
Guide Price: £11

Budget

Hostel (YHA),
Cowgill,
Dent,
Sedbergh,
Cumbria LA10 5RN
Tel: (05875) 251
Guide Price: £5.50

Campsite,
Mrs Irving,
Harbergill Farm,
Cowgill,
Dent,
Sedbergh,
Cumbria LA10 5RG,
Tel: (05875) 392
Guide Price: £1 per tent,
plus 50p per person

Campsite,
Conder Farm,
Dent,
Sedbergh LA10 5QT
Tel: (05875) 277
Guide Price: £2 per person

Dent Town

Hotels/Inns

George & Dragon Hotel,
Dent,
Sedbergh,
Cumbria LA10 5QL
Tel: (05875) 256
Guide Price: £15-£17

The Sun Inn,
Dent,
Dentdale,
Cumbria LA10 5QL
Tel: (05875) 208
Guide Price: £13.50

Guesthouses/B & Bs

G Hudson & P Barber,
Stone Close Tea Shop,
Main Street,

Dent, Sedbergh,
Cumbria LA10 5QL
Tel: (05875) 231
Guide Price: £12.50

Mrs Gunson,
Slack Cottage,
Dent,
Sedbergh,
Cumbria LA10 5QU
Tel: (05875) 439
Guide Price: £9

SEDBERGH

Hotels/Inns

Bull Hotel,
Main Street,
Sedbergh,
Cumbria LA10 5BL
Tel: (05396) 20264
Guide Price: £14.50-£18

Dalesman Country Inn,
Main Street,
Sedbergh,
Cumbria LA10 5BN
Tel: (05396) 21183
Guide Price: £18-£20

Mrs Ingham,
Oakdene Country House Hotel,
Garsdale Road,
Sedbergh,
Cumbria LA10 5JN
Tel: (05396) 20280
Guide Price: £27

Guesthouses/B & Bs

Mrs Jarvis,
The Moss,
Garsdale Road,
Sedbergh,
Cumbria LA10 5JL
Tel: (05396) 20940
Guide Price: £13.50

Mrs Hoggarth,
The Myers,
Joss Lane,
Sedbergh,
Cumbria LA10 5AS
Tel: (05396) 20257
Guide Price: £12

Mr & Mrs Ramsden,
Sun Lea,
Joss Lane,
Sedbergh,
Cumbria LA10 5AS
Tel: (05396) 20828
Guide Price: £11-£13

Mrs Sumner,
Ghyll Farm,
Soolbank,
Sedbergh,
Cumbria LA10 5LJ
Tel: (05396) 20528
Guide Price: £12

Mrs Swainbank,
25 Bainbridge Road,
Sedbergh,
Cumbria LA10 5AU
Tel: (05396) 20685
Guide Price: £11-£12.50

Miss Thurlby,
Stable Antiques,
15 Back Lane,
Sedbergh,
Cumbria LA10 5AQ
Tel: (05396) 20251
Guide Price: £12

Mrs Kerry,
Marshall House,
Main Street,
Sedbergh,
Cumbria LA10 5BL
Tel: (05396) 21053
Guide Price: from £17.50

Mr and Mrs Liddy-Smith,
Turvey House,
Sedbergh,
Cumbria LA10 5DJ
Tel: (05396) 20841
Guide Price: £13

Mr and Mrs Newsham,
Farfield Guest House,
Hawes Road,
Sedbergh,
Cumbria LA10 5LP
Tel: (05396) 20537
Guide Price: £16

Mrs Sharrocks,
Holmecroft,
Station Road,
Sedbergh,
Cumbria LA10 5DW
Tel: (05396) 20754
Guide Price: £13

Mrs Stimson,
Katie Croft,
Garsdale Road,
Sedbergh,
Cumbria LA10 5JL
Tel: (05396) 21038
Guide Price: £13.50

Mrs Snow,
Randall Hill,
Sedbergh,
Cumbria LA10 5HJ
Tel: (05396) 20633
Guide Price: £14

Mrs Dickinson,
Breeze Hill,
39 Guldrey Lane,
Sedbergh,
Cumbria LA10 5DS
Tel: (05396) 21257
Guide Price: £11

Budget

**Campsite,
Borrett Farm,
Sedbergh
Cumbria LA10 5HL
Tel: (05396) 20440
Guide Price: from £3 per tent. Camping & caravan site with showers & toilets. Dairy produce available. Situated on the A683, one mile from Sedbergh town centre. Convenient for Dales Way.**

**Campsite,
Pinfold Caravan Park,
Garsdale Road,
Sedbergh,
Cumbria LA10 5JL
Tel: (05396) 20576
Guide Price: Hikers £2, car tent £5.60. Campsite & caravan park; modern shower & toilet block, laundry, telephone, Calor & 'Gaz. Open March to October 31. Convenient for Lakes & Dales. Sedbergh town approx 500 yards; Kendal 11 miles.**

Campsite,
Lincoln's Inn Farm,
Bridge End,
Sedbergh,
Cumbria
Tel: (05396) 20567
Guide Price: £1 per person

Bunkbarn,
Mrs Handley,
Catholes Farm,
Dent Road,
Sedbergh,
Cumbria LA10 5SS
Tel: (05396) 20334
Guide Price: £4

Kendal, just off the Dales Way, offers a variety of accommodation for walkers.

LUNEDALE

Guesthouses/B & Bs

Mrs Mattinson,
Ash Hining Farm,
Howgill,
Cumbria LA10 5HU
Tel: (05396) 20957
Guide Price: £13

Mrs Hill,
High Branthwaite Farm,
Howgill,
Sedbergh,
Cumbria LA10 5HU
Tel: (05396) 20579
Guide Price: £10-£11

Mrs Middleton,
Davy Bank Mill,
Lowgill,
Crook of Lune,
Cumbria LA10 5HU
Tel: (053984) 241
Guide Price: £10-£11

Mrs Hogg,
Tarnclose,
Beckfoot,
Lowgill,
Cumbria LA8 OBL
Tel: (053984) 658
Guide Price: £11.50

GRAYRIGG

Guesthouses/B & Bs

Mrs Bindloss,
Grayrigg Hall,
Grayrigg,
Cumbria LA8 9BU
Tel: (053984) 689
Guide Price: £11

KENDAL

Guesthouses/B & Bs

Mrs Hill,
29 Sedbergh Road,
Kendal,
Cumbria LA9 6AD
Tel: (0539) 728844
Guide Price: £10

Fairways Guest House,
102 Windermere Road,
Kendal,
Cumbria LA9 5EZ
Tel: (0539) 725564
Guide Price: £15-£18

Fernlea Guest House,
46 Shap Road,
Kendal,
Cumbria LA9 6DP
Tel: (0539) 720402
Guide Price: £13

Kylami Guest House,
11 Burneside Road,
Kendal,
Cumbria LA9 4RL
Tel: (0539) 731198
Guide Price: £10

Meadowbank,
Shap Road,
Kendal,
Cumbria LA9 6NY
Tel: (0539) 721926
Guide Price: £12.50

Rosevale,
60 Shap Road,
Kendal,
Cumbria LA9 6DP
Tel: (0539) 723687
Guide Price: £12

Welton Rise,
44 Shap Road,
Kendal,
Cumbria LA9 6DP
Tel: (0539) 732454
Guide Price: £11-£15

Budget

Hostel (YHA),
Highgate, Kendal,
Cumbria LA9 4HE
Tel: (0539) 724066
Guide Price: £7-£9

BURNESIDE

Guesthouse/B & Bs

Mrs Beaty,
Garnett House Farm,
Burneside,
Kendal,
Cumbria LA9 5SF,
Tel: (0539) 724542
Guide Price: £11.50

Hillfold Farm,
Burneside,
Kendal,
Cumbria LA9 9AU
Tel: (0539) 722574
Guide Price: £11

Hill Farm,
Garnett Bridge Road,
Burneside,
Kendal,
Cumbria LA9 9AU
Tel: (0539) 741273
Guide Price: £10-£11.50

Mrs Ellis,
Gateside Farm,
Burneside,
Kendal,
Cumbria LA9 5SE
Tel: (0539) 722036
Guide Price: £12

STAVELEY

Eagle & Child Hotel,
Kendal Road,
Staveley,
Cumbria LA8 9LP
Tel: (0539) 831320
Guide Price: from £15

Guesthouses/B & Bs

Mr & Mrs Kelly,
Fell View Guest House,

Having reached Bowness, you can sit by Lake Windermere and watch the boats sailing by.

Danes Road,
Staveley,
Cumbria LA8 9PW
Tel: (0539) 821209
Guide Price: £12

H Alexander,
Danes House ,
1 Danes Road,
Staveley,
Cumbria LA8 9PW
Tel: (0539) 821294
Guide Price: £11.50

Hill View,
Kentmere Road,
Staveley,
Cumbria LA8 9JF
Tel: (0539) 821494
Guide Price: £12

Stock Bridge Farm,
Kendal Road,
Staveley,
Cumbria LA8 9LP
Tel: (0539) 821580
Guide Price: £11.50

Budget

Ashes Lane Caravan &
Camping Park,
Staveley,
Near Kendal,
Cumbria LA8 9JS
Tel: (0539) 821110
Guide Price: £5.25 per tent

BOWNESS ON WINDERMERE

Hotels/Inns

White Lodge Hotel,
Lake Road,
Bowness,
Cumbria LA23 2JJ
Tel: (09662) 3624
Guide Price: £24.50

Elim Bank Hotel,
Lake Road,
Bowness,
Cumbria LA23 2JJ
Tel: (09662) 4810
Guide Price: £21

Eastbourne Hotel,
Biskey Howe Road,
Bowness,
Cumbria LA23 3JR
Tel: (09662) 3525
Guide Price: £14-18

Guesthouses/B & Bs

Elim House,
Biskey Howe Road,
Bowness,
Cumbria LA23 2JP
Tel: (09662) 4271
Guide Price: £14

Fell View Guest House,
38 Craig Walk, Bowness,
Cumbria LA23 2JT
Tel: (09662) 5596
Guide Price: £12-£15

Field House,
Belsfield Terrace,
Bowness,
Cumbria LA23 3EQ
Tel: (09662) 2476
Guide Price: £15-£18

Holly Cottages,
Rayrigg Road,
Bowness,
Cumbria LA23 3BZ
Tel: (09662) 4250
Guide Price: £17.50

Holmlea,
Kendal Road,
Bowness,
Cumbria LA23 3EW
Tel: (09662) 2597
Guide Price: £15-£17

Craigwood Guest House,
119 Craig Walk,
Bowness,
Cumbria LA23 3AX
Tel: (09662) 4914
Guide Price: £12-£14

Mrs Shankley,
77 Craig Walk,
Bowness,
Cumbria LA23 2JT
Tel: (09662) 354
Guide Price: £11.50

Brooklands,
Ferry View,
Bowness,
Cumbria LA23 3JB
Tel: (09662) 2344
Guide Price: £16-£18

Brook House,
3 Craig Walk,
Bowness,
Cumbria LA23 2ES
Tel: (09662) 3809
Guide Price: £13.50

Belsfield Guest House,
4 Belsfield Terrace,
Bowness,
Cumbria LA23 3EQ
Tel: (09662) 5823
Guide Price: £18.50-£19

Laurel Cottage,
St Martins Square,
Bowness,
Cumbria LA23 3EF
Tel: (09662) 5594
Guide Price: £18

May Cottage,
Kendal Road,
Bowness,
Cumbria LA23 3EW
Tel: (09662) 6478
Guide Price: £14

New Hall Bank,
Fallbarrow Road,
Bowness,
Cumbria LA23 3DJ
Tel: (09662) 3558
Guide Price: £13-£17

Reflections on Lake Windermere.

Oakfold,
Beresford Road,
Bowness,
Cumbria LA23 2JG
Tel: (09662) 3239
Guide Price: £15

Robins Nest,
1 North Terrace,
Bowness,
Cumbria LA23 3AU
Tel: (09662) 6446
Guide Price: £12

St Johns Lodge,
Lake Road,
Bowness,
Cumbria LA23 2EQ
Tel: (09662) 3078
Guide Price: £18.75

Virginia Cottage,
Kendal Road,
Bowness,
Cumbria LA23 3EJ
Tel: (09662) 4891
Guide Price: £14-£18

Mr & Mrs Garvey,
Field House Guest House,
Kendal Road,
Bowness,
Cumbria LA23 3EQ
Tel: (09662) 2476
Guide Price: £15-£19

SETTLE-CARLISLE WAY

The Settle-Carlisle Way was opened in 1990 by Mike Harding, entertainer and Vice President of the Ramblers' Association. The guidebook to the route is *Settle & Carlisle Country*, by Colin Speakman and John Morrison. The book provides a detailed description of the 140-mile walk from Leeds to the border city of Carlisle, together with maps of the route and photographs of many of the interesting features to be seen along the way.

The building of the Settle-Carlisle line was a triumph of railway engineering: driving a high-speed, high-level line through the Pennine hills. Construction work, including miles of tunnels, bridges and viaducts, was completed in 1876.

The fortunes of this most spectacular railway line plummeted in recent years, and closure was imminent. That it was saved from such an ignominious fate is due largely to the efforts of those who campaigned tirelessly — and successfully — to save the line.

The Settle-Carlisle Way follows — roughly — the course of the line, but deviates sufficiently to include the most interesting walking country. The early part of the walk is along the towpath of the Leeds-Liverpool Canal. The industrial scene is left behind at Skipton, as the route meanders through the limestone scenery of the Yorkshire Dales National Park. Walkers pass the 24 arches of the Ribblehead viaduct: argu-

An annual sheep fair is held at Ribblehead, within sight of the famous viaduct.

ably the finest piece of railway engineering on the line.

Past the bleak yet beautiful Mallerstang valley, the walk and railway then follow the meanderings of the lovely River Eden, with its picturesque villages of sandstone houses, until Carlisle comes into view.

The Settle-Carlisle Way is, naturally enough, of special interest to railway enthusiasts, though the route takes in a host of other features too, such as limestone pavements, tiny Dales villages, historic castles, drovers' roads, rushing waterfalls and even a splendid stone circle called Long Meg and her Daughters.

The walk is split into ten sections, each of which can be covered by fit walkers in a day. The sections begin and end at one of the railway stations on the line and, in most cases, a town or village where overnight accommodation can be had. So the walk can be tackled in a single ten-day stretch, or taken a stage at a time by using the railway at the beginning and end of a day's walk.

Walkers will need a copy of *Settle & Carlisle Country*, because the route is not waymarked.

These are the ten stages of the Settle-Carlisle Way, with daily mileages:

Leeds to Saltaire (14)
Saltaire to Skipton (16)
Skipton to Settle (14)
Settle to Ribblehead (15)
Ribblehead to Garsdale (9)
Garsdale to Kirkby Stephen (13)
Kirkby Stephen to Appleby (15)
Appleby to Langwathby (13)
Langwathby to Armathwaite (13)
Armathwaite to Carlisle (14)

CARLISLE
Armathwaite
Lazonby
Langwathby
Appleby
Kirkby Stephen
Garsdale
Dent
Ribblehead
Horton in Ribblesdale
Settle
Long Preston
Hellifield
Gargrave
Clitheroe
Skipton
Cononley
Steeton
Keighley
Bingley
Crossflats
Saltaire
Shipley
Frizinghall
Bradford
LEEDS

LEEDS

Hotels/Inns

The Aintree Hotel,
38 Cardigan Road,
Headingley,
Leeds,
W Yorks
Tel: (0532) 758290
Guide Price: £19.50

Ashfield Hotel,
44 Cardigan Road,
Headingley,
Leeds,
W Yorks
Tel: (0532) 758847
Guide Price: £19.50-£33

SHIPLEY

Hotels/Inns

Sun Hotel,
3 Kirkgate,
Shipley,
West Yorks
Tel: (0274) 589159
Guide Price: £12.50

Homeleigh Hotel,
74/76 Bradford Road,
Shipley,
West Yorks
Tel: (0274) 584818
Guide Price: £34

Kirkstall Abbey is a landmark familiar to travellers leaving Leeds on a Carlisle train.

The five-rise locks at Bingley are one of the best-known features to be seen on the Leeds-Liverpool Canal.

Guesthouses/B & Bs

Cliffwood Guest House,
1 Cliffe Wood Avenue,
Shipley,
West Yorks
Tel: (0274) 591664
Guide Price: £11-£16

Clifton Guest House,
75 Kirkgate,
Shipley,
West Yorks
Tel: (0274) 580509
Guide Price: £19-£25

Northern Guest House,
62 Kirkgate,
Shipley,
West Yorks
Tel: (0274) 583854
Guide Price: £17

BINGLEY

Midland Hotel,
148 Main Street,
Bingley,
W Yorks BD16 2HZ
Tel: (0274) 563124
Guide Price: £17

B & B,
4 Crosley View,
Gilstead,
Bingley,
W Yorks BD16 4QZ
Tel: (0274) 567270
Guide Price: from £9

KEIGHLEY

The Beeches Hotel,
Bradford Road,
Keighley,
West Yorks
Tel: (0535) 607227
Guide Price:

Airedale Guest House,
70 Devonshire Street,
Keighley,
West Yorks
Tel: (0535) 607597
Guide Price: £13

CONONLEY

B & B,
Mrs Smith,
High View,
Windle Lane,

Cononley,
Skipton,
N Yorks BD20 8JT
Tel: (0535) 632815
Guide Price: £14-£15

SKIPTON

Hotels/Inns

Herriots Hotel,
Broughton Road,
Skipton,
N Yorks BD23 1RT
Tel: (0756) 792781
Guide Price: £28

Highfield Hotel,
58 Keighley Road,
Skipton,
N Yorks BD23 2NB
Tel: (0756) 793182
Guide Price: £17-£18

Guesthouses/B & Bs

Mrs Hundsdoerfer,
Craven Heifer Farm,
Grassington Road,
Skipton,
N Yorks BD23 3LA
Tel: (0756) 793732
Guide Price: £13

Mr & Mrs Milnes,
Bourne House,
22 Upper Sackville Street,
Skipton,
N Yorks BD23 2EB
Tel: (0756) 792633
Guide Price: £13

Mrs Parkinson,
Aire Dale View,
26 Belle View Terrace,
Broughton Road,
Skipton,
N Yorks BD23 1RU
Tel: (0756) 791195
Guide Price: £13

Mrs Rushton,
Craven House,
56 Keighley Road,
Skipton,
N Yorks BD23 2WB
Tel: (0756) 794657
Guide Price: £14

Mrs Wright,
1 Salisbury Street,
Skipton,
N Yorks BD23 1NQ
Tel: (0756) 791135
Guide Price: £14

Narrow-boats tied up at Gargrave lock.

GARGRAVE

Kirk Syke Hotel,
19 High Street,
Gargrave,
Skipton,
North Yorks BD23 3RA.
Tel: (0756) 749356
Guide Price: £25

Guesthouses/B & Bs

Mrs Greenwood,
The Coppice,
31 Skipton Road,
Gargrave,
Skipton,
North Yorks BD23 3SA.
Tel: (0756) 749335
Guide Price: £10-£11

Mrs Moorhouse,
2 Westville Gardens,
Eshton Road,
Gargrave,
Skipton,
N Yorks BD23 3SE
Tel: (0756) 748084
Guide Price: £11

Mr & Mrs Shelmerdine,
Eshton Grange,
Gargrave,
Skipton,
N Yorks BD23 3QE
Tel: (0756) 749383
Guide Price: £17-£19

BELL BUSK

B & B,
Mrs Philpott,
Tudor House,
Bell Busk,
Skipton,
N Yorks BD23 4DT
Tel: (07293) 301
Guide Price: £14

AIRTON

B & B,
Mrs Robinson,
Lindon House,
Airton,
Skipton,
N Yorks BD23 4BE
Tel: (07293) 418
Guide Price: £16.50

HELLIFIELD

Black Horse Hotel,
Main Road,
Hellifield,
Skipton,
N Yorks BD23 4HT
Tel: (07295) 223
Guide Price: £25

B & B,
Mrs Phillip,
Wenningber Farm,
Hellifield,
Skipton,
N Yorks BD23 4JR
Tel: (07295) 856
Guide Price: £13

LONG PRESTON

Hotels/Inns

Boars Head Hotel,
Long Preston,
Skipton,
N Yorks
Tel: (07294) 217
Guide Price: £20

Maypole Inn,
Long Preston,
Skipton,
N Yorks BD23 4PH
Tel: (07294) 219
Guide Price: £14.50

SETTLE

Hotels/Inns

Falcon Manor,
Skipton Road,
Settle,
N Yorks BD24 9BD
Tel: (0729) 823814
Guide Price: from £34

Royal Oak Hotel,
Market Place,
Settle,
N Yorks BD24 9ED
Tel: (0729) 822561
Guide Price: £37.90

Guesthouse/B & Bs

Yorkshire Rose Guest House,
1 The Terrace,
Duke Street,
Settle,
N Yorks
Tel: (0729) 822032
Guide Price: £15

Mr & Mrs Beecroft,
Penmar Court,
Duke Street,
Settle,
N Yorks BD24 9HS
Tel: (0729) 823258
Guide Price: £12-£13

Mrs King,
The Oast Guest House,
5 Penyghent View,
Settle,
N Yorks BD24 9JJ
Tel: (0729) 822989
Guide Price: £13.50-£17.50

Mrs Norris,
Halsteads,
3 Halsteads Terrace,
Duke Street,
Settle,
N Yorks BD24 9AP
Tel: (0729) 822823
Guide Price: £15.50-£19

Mrs Skirrow,
Primrose House,
Victoria Street,
Settle,
N Yorks BD24 9EY
Tel: (0729) 823682
Guide Price: £12.50

Miss Wall,
Whitefriars Guest House,
Church Street,
Settle,
N Yorks BD24 9JD
Tel: (0729) 823753
Guide Price: £14.50-£18

LANGCLIFFE

Bowerley Hotel,
Langcliffe,
Settle,
N Yorks BD24 9LY
Tel: (0729) 823811
Guide Price: £18-£23

STAINFORTH

B & B,
Mrs Woodmansey,
Townhead Farmhouse,
Stainforth,
Settle,
N Yorks BD24 9PJ
Tel: (0729) 823181
Guide Price: £11

Hostel (YHA),
Taitlands,
Stainforth,
Settle,
N Yorks BD24 9PA
Tel: (0729) 823577
Guide Price: £5.90

Pen-y-Ghent, one of the famous Three Peaks.

HORTON IN RIBBLESDALE

Hotels/Inns

Mr Johnson,
The Golden Lion Hotel,
Horton-in-Ribblesdale,
Settle,
N Yorks
Tel: (07296) 206
Guide Price: £15

Mr & Mrs Hargreaves,
The Crown Inn,
Horton-in-Ribblesdale,
N Yorks BD24 OHF
Tel: (07296) 209
Guide Price: £13.70-£18.70

Guesthouses/B & Bs

**Mr & Mrs Jowett,
Burnside,
Horton-in-Ribblesdale,
Settle,
N Yorks BD24 OEX
Tel: (07296) 223
Guide Price: £12-£14**

Mr & Mrs Jones,
The Rowe House,
Horton-in-Ribblesdale,
Settle, N Yorks BD24 OHT
Tel: (07296) 212
Guide Price: £16.50-£22

Mrs Kenyon,
South House Farm,
Horton-in-Ribblesdale,
Settle,
N Yorks BD24 OHU
Tel: (07296) 271
Guide Price: £11

Mr & Mrs Rhodes,
Waltergarth,
Station Road,
Horton-in-Ribblesdale,
Settle,
N Yorks BD24 OHH
Tel: (07296) 221
Guide Price: £12.50

Mrs Barker,
The Willows,
Horton-in-Ribblesdale,
Settle, N Yorks
Tel: (07296) 373
Guide Price: £12-£15

Mr & Mrs Horsfall,
Studfold House,
Horton-in-Ribblesdale,
Settle,
N Yorks
Tel: (07296) 200
Guide Price: £12

Wagi's Guest House,
Townend Cottage,
Horton-in-Ribblesdale,
Settle,
N Yorks
Tel: (07296) 320
Guide Price: £13

Mrs Pilkington,
Middle Studfold Farm,
Horton-in-Ribblesdale,
Settle,
N Yorks BD24 0ER
Tel: (07296) 236
Guide Price: £12

Budget

Bunkhouse,
Mrs Glasgow,
Dub Cote Farm,
Horton-in-Ribblesdale,
Settle,
N Yorks
Tel: (07296)238
Guide Price: £4.50

SELSIDE

B & B,
Mr & Mrs Wormington,
Top Farm,
Selside,
Settle,
N Yorks BD24 0HZ
Tel: (07296) 370
Guide Price: £12.50-£16

RIBBLEHEAD

Station Inn,
Ribblehead,
Nr Ingleton,
N Yorks LA6 3AS
Tel: (05242) 41274
Guide Price: £12 (also bunkbarn: £4 per person)

B & B and campsite,
Mrs Timmins,
Gearstones,
Ribblehead,
Ingleton,
N Yorks LA6 3AS
Tel: (0468) 41405
Guide Price: £10.50

DENTDALE

Hotels/Inns

Sportsman's Inn,
Cowgill,
Dent,
Sedbergh,
Cumbria LA10 5RG
Tel: (05875) 282
Guide Price: from £14.30

Guesthouses/B & Bs

Mrs Hunter,
Rash House,
Dent Foot,
Dentdale,
Cumbria LA10 5SU
Tel: (05396) 20113
Guide Price: £11.50

Mrs Parkes,
Carley Hall Cottage,
Cowgill,
Dentdale,
Cumbria LA10 5RL
Tel: (05875) 244
Guide Price: £11.50

Sunlight picks out the cobbles in Dent, a village of white-washed houses and great character.

Mrs Ferguson,
Scow Cottage,
Dent Head,
Dentdale,
Cumbria LA10 5RN
Tel: (05875) 445
Guide Price: £11

Budget

Hostel (YHA),
Cowgill,
Dent,
Sedbergh,
Cumbria LA10 5RN
Tel: (05875) 251
Guide Price: £5.50

Campsite,
Mrs Irving,
Harbergill Farm,
Cowgill,
Dent,
Sedbergh,
Cumbria LA10 5RG,
Tel: (05875) 392
Guide Price: £1 per tent,
plus 50p per person

Campsite,
Conder Farm,
Dent,
Sedbergh LA10 5QT
Tel: (05875) 277
Guide Price: £2 per person

Dent Town

Hotels/Inns

George & Dragon Hotel,
Dent,
Sedbergh,
Cumbria LA10 5QL
Tel: (05875) 256
Guide Price: £15-£17

The Sun Inn,
Dent,
Cumbria LA10 5QL
Tel: (05875) 208
Guide Price: £13.50

Guesthouses/B & Bs

G Hudson & P Barber,
Stone Close Tea Shop,
Main Street,
Dent,
Sedbergh,
Cumbria LA10 5QL
Tel: (05875) 231
Guide Price: £12.50

Mrs Gunson,
Slack Cottage,
Dent,
Sedbergh,
Cumbria LA10 5QU
Tel: (05875) 439
Guide Price: £9

GARSDALE HEAD

The Moorcock Inn,
Garsdale,
Sedbergh,
Cumbria
Tel: (0969) 667488
Guide Price: £15

Guesthouses/B & Bs

Mr & Mrs Todd,
Blades Farm,
Garsdale,
Sedbergh,
Cumbria LA10 5PF
Tel: (05396) 20615
Guide Price: £10-£12

Mrs Harper,
Brookside,
Garsdale Head,
Sedbergh,
Cumbria LA10 5PW
Tel: (05396) 20632
Guide Price: £11

Pendragon Castle, now merely a picturesque ruin, is reputed to have been the birthplace of King Arthur.

Mrs Joanne Cox,
East Mudbecks,
Garsdale Head,
Sedbergh,
Cumbria
Tel: (05396) 21328
Guide Price: £12

Mrs Naysmith,
Cocklake House,
Near Outhgill,
Mallerstang,
Cumbria CA17 4JT
Tel: (07683) 72908
Guide Price: £14-£15

MALLERSTANG

Guesthouses/B & Bs

Pauline Hasted,
Aisgill Crafts,
Mallerstang,
Kirkby Stephen,
Cumbria
Tel: (07683) 72011
Guide Price: £11.50

Sheelagh Sawyer,
Ing Hill,
Mallerstang,
Kirkby Stephen,
Cumbria
Tel: (07683) 71153
Guide Price: £20

KIRKBY STEPHEN

Hotels/Inns

Croglin Castle Hotel,
South Road,
Kirkby Stephen,
Cumbria CA17 4SY
Tel: (07683) 71389
Guide Price: £12

Black Bull Hotel,
Kirkby Stephen,
Cumbria CA17 4QN
Tel: (07683) 71237
Guide Price: £13

Guesthouses/B & Bs

Mrs Claxton,
The Old Court House,
High Street,
Kirkby Stephen,
Cumbria CA17 4SH
Tel: (07683) 71061
Guide Price: £12.50

Jolly Farmer's Guest House,
63 High Street,
Kirkby Stephen,
Cumbria CA17 4SH
Tel: (07683) 71063
Guide Price: £12.50

Mrs Crowson,
Sower Pow,
Victoria Square,
Kirkby Stephen,
Cumbria CA17 4QA
Tel: (07683) 71030
Guide Price: £12.50

Mrs Robinson,
Barium House,
Nateby Road,
Kirkby Stephen,
Cumbria
Tel: (07683) 71095
Guide Price: £12

Mrs Dean,
Brougham House,
Kirkby Stephen,
Cumbria CA17 4SH
Tel: (07683) 71324
Guide Price: £15-£18

Town Head House,
High Street,
Kirkby Stephen,
Cumbria CA17 4SH
Tel: (07683) 71044
Guide Price: £34

Mrs Prime,
Redmayne House,
Silver Street,
Kirkby Stephen,
Cumbria CA17 4RB
Tel: (07683) 71441
Guide Price: £12.50

Mrs Rogan,
Standards Villa,
58 South Road,
Kirkby Stephen,
Cumbria CA17 4SN
Tel: (07683) 72138
Guide Price: £12

Mrs Bradwell,
Fletcher House,
Kirkby Stephen, Cumbria
CA17 4QQ
Tel: (07683) 71013
Guide Price: £15

Mr & Mrs Hughes,
Redenol House,
56 South Road,
Kirkby Stephen
Cumbria CA17 4SN
Tel: (07683) 71489
Guide Price: £12

**Annedd Gwyon,
46 High Street,
Kirkby Stephen,
Cumbria CA17 4SH
Tel: (07683) 72302
Guide Price: £12-15**

Winton Manor Farmhouse,
Winton,
Kirkby Stephen,
Cumbria CA17 4ML
Tel: (07683) 71255
Guide Price: £12.50

Budget

Campsite,
Pennine View Caravan

Park,
Station Road,
Kirkby Stephen,
Cumbria CA17 4SZ
Tel: (07683) 71717
Guide Price: £2 per person

Hostel (YHA),
Fletcher Hill,
Market Street,
Kirkby Stephen,
Cumbria CA17 4QQ
Tel: (07683) 71793
Guide Price: from £4

CROSBY GARRETT

Mr & Mrs Dewhirst,
Chestnut House,
Crosby Garrett,
Kirkby Stephen,
Cumbria CA17 4PR
Tel: (07683) 71230
Guide Price: £11

Campsite,
Wild Rose Park,
Ormside,
Appleby,
Cumbria CA16 6WJ
Tel: (07683) 51077
Guide Price: £6-£9

SOULBY

Guesthouses/B & Bs

Mrs A E March,
Hutton Lodge, Soulby,
Kirkby Stephen,
Cumbria CA17 4PL
Tel: (07683) 71396
Guide Price: £12-£14

Mrs Sayer,
Syke Side Farm,
Soulby,
Kirkby Stephen,
Cumbria CA17 4PJ
Tel: (07683) 71137
Guide Price: £9

The High Cross in Boroughgate, Appleby, was built to show the limit of the market.

The Old Vicarage,
Soulby,
Kirkby Stephen,
Cumbria CA17 4PL
Tel: (07683) 71477
Guide Price: £13

APPLEBY

Midland Hotel,
25 Clifford Street,
Appleby,
Cumbria CA16 6TS
Tel: (07683) 51524
Guide Price: £15

Guesthouses/B & Bs

The Friary,
Battlebarrow,
Appleby,
Cumbria CA16 6XT
Tel: (07683) 52702
Guide Price: £17-£20

Mrs M Wood,
Gale House Farm,
Roman Road,
Appleby,
Cumbria CA16 6JB
Tel: (07683) 51380
Guide Price: £11

Howgill House,
Bongate
Appleby,
Cumbria CA16 6UW
Tel: (07683) 51574
Guide Price: £10.50

Kirkber Farm,
Appleby,
Cumbria CA16 6JG
Tel: (07683) 51389
Guide Price: £12

Mrs Coward,
Limnerslease,
Bongate,
Appleby,
Cumbria CA16 6UE,
Tel: (07683) 51578
Guide Price: £12

Mrs Dayson,
Bongate House,
Appleby,
Cumbria CA16 6UE
Guide Price: £13.50-£16

DUFTON

Guesthouses/B & Bs

Mrs Burrows,
Bow Hall,
Dufton,
Appleby,
Cumbria
Tel: (07683) 51835
Guide Price: £12.50

Mrs Howe,
Dufton Hall Farm,
Dufton,
Appleby,
Cumbria CA16 6DD
Tel: (07683) 51573
Guide Price: £12

Mrs M A Hullock,
Ghyll View,
Dufton,
Appleby,
Cumbria CA16 6DB
Tel: (07683) 51855
Guide Price: £10.50

Budget

Campsite,
Brow Farm,
Dufton,
Appleby,
Cumbria CA16 6DF

This stone circle, known as Long Meg and her Daughters, is a fascinating Neolithic site near Langwathby.

Tel: (07683) 51202
Guide Price: £1

Campsite,
Silverband Park,
Silverband,
Knock,
Near Appleby,
Cumbria CA16 6DL,
Tel: (07683) 61218
Guide Price: £5

Hostel (YHA),
"Redstones",
Dufton,
Appleby,
Cumbria CA16 6DB
Guide Price: £4

KIRKBY THORE

B & B,
Banker House,
Kirkby Thore,
Penrith,
Cumbria CA 10 1XN
Tel: (07683) 61166
Guide Price: £12-£17.50

LANGWATHBY

Guesthouses/B & Bs

Cross Fell View,
Langwathby,
Penrith,
Cumbria CA10 1NW
Tel: (0768) 881463
Guide Price: £12

Mrs McDonnell,
The Old Vicarage,
Edenhall,
Langwathby,
Penrith,
Cumbria CA11 8SX
Tel: (0768) 881329
Guide Price: £13-£15

Home Farm,
Edenhall,
Near Langwathby,
Penrith,
Cumbria
Tel: (0768) 881203
Guide Price: £12

Carlisle: the end of the line for Settle-Carlisle Wayfarers and train travellers.

LAZONBY

Banktop House,
Lazonby,
Penrith,
Cumbria CA10 1AJ
Tel: (076883):268
Guide Price: £12

KIRKOSWALD

Hotels/Inns

The Fetherston Arms,
Kirkoswald,
Penrith,
Cumbria CA10 1DQ
Tel: (076883) 284
Guide Price: £14

The Nunnery House Hotel,
Staffield,
Kirkoswald,
Penrith,
Cumbria CA10 1EU
Tel: (076883) 537
Guide Price: £14-£30

B & B,
Crossfield Farm,
Kirkoswald,
Penrith,
Cumbria CA10 1EU
Tel: (076883) 711
Guide Price: £11-£15

ARMATHWAITE

Dukes Head Hotel,
Front Street,
Armathwaite, Carlisle,
Cumbria CA4 9PB
Tel: (06992) 226
Guide Price: £20

Fox and Pheasant Inn,
Armathwaite,
Carlisle,
Cumbria CA4 9PY
Tel: (06992) 400
Guide Price: £18

Guesthouses/B & Bs

Low Fauld Farm,
Ruckcroft,
Armathwaite,
Carlisle,
Cumbria CA4 9QS
Tel: (076886) 241
Guide Price: £10

Mrs Brown,
Quarry House,
Armathwaite,
Carlisle,
Cumbria CA4 9SL
Tel: (06992) 282
Guide Price: £7.50

WETHERAL

Killoran Hotel,
The Green,
Wetheral,
Carlisle,
Cumbria CA4 8ET
Tel: (0228) 560200
Guide Price: £20

CARLISLE

The Royal Hotel,
Lowther Street,
Carlisle,
Cumbria
0228 22103
Guide Price: £15.50

The Angus Hotel,
14 Scotland Road,
Carlisle,
Cumbria CA3 9DG
Tel: (0228) 23546
Guide Price: £14-£26

Guesthouses/B & Bs

Averley Villa Guest House,
122 Warwick Road,
Carlisle,
Cumbria CA1 1LF
Tel: (0228) 34074
Guide Price: £13-£15

The Beeches,
Wood Street,
Carlisle,
Cumbria CA1 2SF
Tel: (0228) 511962
Guide Price: £13

Calreena Guest House,
123 Warwick Road,
Carlisle,
Cumbria CA1 1JZ
Tel: (0228) 25020
Guide Price: £11

Cartref,
44 Victoria Place,
Carlisle,
Cumbria CA1 1EY
Tel: (0228) 22077
Guide Price: £12

Chatsworth Guest House,
22 Chatsworth Square,
Carlisle,
Cumbria CA1 1HF
Tel: (0228) 24023
Guide Price: £12-£15

Corner House,
87 Petteril Street,
Carlisle,
Cumbria CA1 2AW
Tel: (0228) 41942

Guide Price: £12-£14
East View Guest House,
110 Warwick Road,
Carlisle,
Cumbria CA1 1JU
Tel: (0228) 22112
Guide Price: £11

Redruth Guest House,
46 Victoria Place,
Carlisle,
Cumbria CA1 1EX
Tel: (0228) 21631
Guide Price: from £15

Langleigh Guest House,
6 Howard Place,
Carlisle,
Cumbria CA1 1HR
Tel: (0228) 30440,
Guide Price: from £15

Mrs Fisher,
Howard House,
27 Howard Place,
Carlisle,
Cumbria CA1 1HR
Tel: (0228) 29159
Guide Price: £12-£15

Basco-Dyke Head Farm,
Ainstable,
Carlisle,
Cumbria
Tel: (076886) 254
Guide Price: £10.50

Marchmain Guest House,
151 Warwick Road,
Carlisle,
Cumbria CA1 1LU
Tel: (0228) 29551
Guide Price: £12

19 Aglionby Street,
Carlisle,
Cumbria CA1 1LE
Tel: (0228) 24566
Guide price: £13-£15

Aidan View Guest House,
154 Warwick Road,
Carlisle,
Cumbria CA1 1LG
Tel: (0228) 32353
Guide Price: £11-£12

Budget

Hostel (YHA),
Etterby House,
Etterby,
Carlisle,
Cumbria CA3 9QS
Tel: (0228) 23934
Guide Price: £3.70

Settle-Carlisle Country

by Colin Speakman and John Morrison

Settle-Carlisle Country is a comprehensive guide to the Settle-Carlisle Way, a 150-mile walk from Leeds to the border city.

The route is divided into ten stages, each of which can be tackled by fit walkers in a day. There is a detailed description of the route, backed up by maps.

The walk passes through some splendid countryside, particularly the Yorkshire Dales and the Eden Valley. The text and the selection of photographs detail many of the fascinating features to be seen along the way, while the introduction provides a short history of what is arguably the most scenic railway line in the country.

Settle-Carlisle Country also contains ten walks that begin and end at stations on the line, allowing walkers to enjoy the countryside while leaving the car at home.

Settle-Carlisle Country
is available from your bookshop or direct from
Leading Edge (GNW), Old Chapel,
Burtersett, Hawes,
North Yorkshire DL8 3PB
Price £5.95 plus 75p P & P

Also: Settle-Carlisle Way completion certificates,
£2 inc postage

Use our credit card ordering service,
or write or phone for our up-to-date catalogue.
(0969) 667566

Other books with an outdoor theme from *Leading Edge*

Touching Cloudbase, by Ian Currer and Rob Cruickshank, is the complete guide to paragliding — one of the fastest-growing and most exhilarating sports in Europe. The authors, both experienced paragliding instructors, give the budding flier the low-down on how to get through basic training and master the art of soaring flight.

The Off-Road Bicycle Book, by Iain Lynn, covers all aspects of this increasingly popular activity. You can learn about the different kinds of all-terrain bikes, how to get the best out of the sport and enjoy one of the many routes detailed in the text. The first edition sold out quickly; this second edition keeps the information bang up to date.

Both these books are available from
your bookshop, or direct from
Leading Edge (GNW), Old Chapel,
Burtersett, Hawes,
North Yorkshire DL8 3PB

Touching Cloudbase, price £6.95 (plus £75p P & P)
The Off-Road Bike Book, price £4.95 (plus £75p P & P)

Use our credit card ordering service, or write or phone for our latest catalogue
(0969) 667566

REFERENCE

PENNINE WAY

Books

Pennine Way Companion, by A Wainwright, published by Westmorland Gazette Ltd, £7.95.

National Trail Guide: Pennine Way, by Tony Hopkins, published by Aurum Press, £7.95
Book 1: Edale to Bowes
Book 2: Bowes to Kirk Yetholm

A Guide to the Pennine Way, by Christopher John Wright, published by Constable, £7.95.

The Pennine Way Pub Guide by Chris Harrison, published by Scarthin Books, price £3.90.

Wainwright on the Pennine Way, published by Mermaid Books, £11.95.

Great Walks: The Pennine Way, by Frank Duerden, published by Ward Lock, £16.95.

The Pennine Way, route-finding maps by Footprint, £2.95 each
Part 1: Edale to Teesdale
Part 2: Teesdale to Kirk Yetholm

The Pennine Way Accommodation Guide, published by the Pennine Way Council, and available by post (price 60p plus A5 SAE) from the editor: John Needham, 23 Woodland Crescent, Hilton Park, Prestwich, Manchester M25 8WQ. The guide also includes information about suitable clothing & footwear, availability of food, banks, transport, etc.

Transport

The Pennine Way was not designed for easy access to public transport, but the following information — and contact phone numbers — may be helpful.
Edale: trains to Sheffield and Manchester (booking office Manchester 061-8328353).
Crowden: buses to Manchester & Sheffield (061-2362120).
Marsden: trains between Manchester, Huddersfield and Leeds.
Stanedge: buses between Huddersfield and Oldham.
Hebden Bridge: trains between Liverpool, Manchester and Leeds.
Cowling: coach service (0535-33823).
Thornton-in-Craven: coaches between Burnley and Skipton (0756-749215).
Gargrave: buses to Skipton, Settle & Malham (0756-749215).
Horton-in-Ribblesdale: buses to Settle (07292-3235), and trains to Leeds and Carlisle.
Hawes: buses (0325-468771) to Leyburn, and bus link to Garsdale station.
Swaledale: buses to Richmond (0325-468771).
Middleton-in-Teesdale: buses (0325-468771).

FROM A WALK IN THE PARK, TO A WALK IN THE ARCTIC... WE'VE GOT THE GEAR

Join the adventurers' in their choice of clothing and equipment.

We offer the widest range of gear - for every occasion - from the conquest of the Arctic, to quiet country walks.

Everything for the traveller from Footwear to Maps right through to Tents and Camping equipment - and much much more!

Friendly surroundings, helpful staff and the widest selection of gear - that's what makes us the UK's number one specialist retailer.

FOR DETAILS OF YOUR NEAREST STORE PHONE 0784 458625 (24 HOURS)

Dufton: nearest railway station is Appleby, for Settle-Carlisle line.
Alston: bus service to Langwathby on S-C line (0228-812812), and buses to Newcastle.
Greenhead: buses to Newcastle & Carlisle (0228-48484).
Byrness: buses between Newcastle & Edinburgh (031-556 8464).
Kirk Yetholm: bus service to Kelso (0573-24141).

Pennine Way walkers should arm themselves with the following 1:50,000 scale OS maps: 74 Kelso; 80 Cheviot Hills; 86 Haltwhistle & Bewcastle; 91 Appleby; 92 Barnard Castle & Richmond; 98 Wensleydale and Wharfedale; 103 Blackburn & Burnley; 109 Manchester and 110 Sheffield & Huddersfield. The following 1:25,000 Outdoor Leisure maps will also be useful: The Dark Peak, South Pennines, Yorkshire Dales (Northern and Central) and Teesdale.

One-inch OS Maps needed:
Sheet 102 Huddersfield
101 Manchester
95 Blackburn & Burnley
90 Wensleydale
84 Teesdale
83 Penrith
77 Hexham
76 Carlisle
71 Alnwick
70 Jedbergh

Tourist Information Centres

Glossop (0457) 855920
Hebden Bridge (0422) 843831
Haworth (0535) 642329
Skipton (0756) 792809
Settle (0792) 823617
Horton-in-Ribblesdale (07296) 333
Hawes (0969) 667450
Brough (09304) 260
Appleby (07683) 51177
Alston (0434) 381696
Haltwhistle (0498) 20351
Once Brewed (04984) 396
Hexham (0434) 605225
Kelso (0573) 23464

The Pennine Way Council exists to promote and protect the Pennine Way; for £2.50 you can become an Associate Member. You will receive a spring and autumn newsletter and a copy of the latest Pennine Way Accommodation and Camping Guide.

Pennine Way Council,
Sec Chris Sainty,
29 Springfield Park Avenue,
Chelmsford,
Essex CM2 6EL

The Youth Hostels Association has a number of hostels along the Pennine Way. The YHA runs (for members only) a central booking service — The Pennine Way Bureau — which enables walkers to book hostel accommodation in advance with just a single letter to the bureau.

For details about this service, in a useful guide book to the Pennine Way and its hostels, send £1.50 to the Pennine Way Bureau, c/o YHA Northern Regional Office, Bowey House, William Street, Newcastle-upon-Tyne NE3 1SA, tel (091) 221 2101.

COAST TO COAST WALK

BOOKS

A Coast to Coast Walk, by A Wainwright, published by Westmorland Gazette Ltd, £7.95.

Wainwright's Coast to Coast Walk, published by Michael Joseph, £15.99.

Accommodation Guides:

The Coast to Coast Walk Accommodation Guide, published by North York Moors Adventure Centre, Park House, Ingleby Cross, Northallerton, N Yorks. Tel: (060982) 571. Price £1.50. Also available are embroidered badges, sweat shirts, T-shirts and Coast to Coast completion certificates.

The Coast to Coast Bed & Breakfast Accommodation Guide is compiled by Mrs Doreen Whitehead, and is available direct from her (£1.50 plus SAE) at East Stonesdale Farm, Keld, Richmond, N Yorks DL11 6LJ.

Tourist Information Centres

Whitehaven (0946) 5678
Grasmere (09665) 245
Glenridding (08532) 414
Kirkby Stephen (07683) 71199
Reeth (0748) 84373
Richmond (0748) 850252
Whitby (0947) 602674

Outdoor Equipment Specialists

Equipment hire
Childrens' gear
Discount on bulk orders
Talks/slide shows
Repairs
Maps & Books

Open Monday to Saturday
120a Blackmoorfoot Road,
Crosland Moor,
Huddersfield HD4 5RL
Tel: (0484) 653997

Trek Sense

THE NORTH EAST'S LEADING STOCKISTS OF
HEAVY DUTY SURVIVAL GEAR & ACCESSORIES

Open Wednesday Afternoon

The items we stock are assessed as being the best available

Survival Rations ✱ Stoves ✱ Survival Kits ✱ Bivvie
Buffalo Four Seasons ✱ Sleeping Bags ✱ Jack Wolfskin
Walking Boots: Helly-Hanson, Hitec & Hawkins
Coming soon: Ultimate clothing and tents
Plus 100s of hard-to-find quality items

198 Northgate
Darlington
Co Durham DL1 1RB
Tel: (0325) 358216

CLEVELAND WAY

BOOKS

Walking the Cleveland Way by Malcolm Boyes, published by Cicerone Press, £5.50.

National Trail Guide: Cleveland Way, by Ian Sampson, published by Aurum Press, £7.95.

Cleveland Way Companion, by Paul Hannon, published by Hillside Publications, £3.45.

A Guide to the Cleveland Way, by Richard Sale, published by Constable, £7.95.

The Cleveland Way, by Bill Cowley, published by Dalesman Books, £3.95.

Tourist Information Centres

Helmsley (70173)
Sutton Bank (0845) 597426
Great Ayton (0642) 722835
Guisborough (0287) 33801
Saltburn (0287) 22422
Staithes (0947) 841251
Whitby (0947) 602674
Robin Hoods Bay (0947) 880512
Ravenscar (0723) 870138
Scarborough (0723) 373333
Filey (0723) 512204

Maps required:
Outdoor Leisure Map: North York Moors (western and eastern areas). Pathfinder TA08/09/18 Scarborough.

DALES WAY

BOOKS

Dales Way Route Guide by Arthur Gemmell and Colin Speakman, published by Stile Publications, £2.20

The Dales Way Companion, by Paul Hannon, published by Hillside Publications, price £3.95.

The Dales Way, by Colin Speakman, published by Dalesman Books, £3.95.

The Dales Way Handbook, published by the West Riding Area of the Ramblers' Association, and available from them at 27 Cookridge Avenue, Leeds LS16 7NA. It includes accommodation listing, transport details, facilities and places of interest, and information about books and maps.

Tourist Information Centres

Otley (0943) 465151
Ilkley (0943) 602319
Grassington (0756) 752774
Sedbergh (05396) 21025
Kendal (0539) 725758

Maps: of the 1:50,000 maps, sheets 104 Leeds & Bradford, 98 Wensleydale and Wharfedale and 97 Kendal & Morecambe will be needed. Or use Outdoor Leisure Maps: Yorkshire Dales Southern Area, Yorkshire Dales Northern & Central Areas, and The English Lakes South-East.

Transport

Regular buses from Leeds to Ilkley (0532-457676), plus a less regular service up Wharfedale as far as Buckden. Buses from Sedbergh and Windermere go to Kendal and Oxenholme station (a couple of miles from Kendal).

Dales Way walkers can take trains on the Settle-Carlisle line — at Dent and Ribblehead (though only southbound trains now stop at Ribblehead station).

SETTLE-CARLISLE WAY

BOOKS

Settle-Carlisle Country, by Colin Speakman and John Morrison, published by Leading Edge, £5.95.

Also available from the publishers: Settle-Carlisle Way completion certificates: £2. T-shirts: full colour, in S, M, L, Extra L and child's sizes, featuring the RailTrail logo. Price £6 (child's size: £5). Mugs, also featuring the RailTrail logo: £2.95 These prices include postage and packing.

Tourist Information Centres:

Leeds (0532) 462816
Skipton (0756) 792809
Settle (0792) 823617
Horton-in-Ribblesdale (07296) 333
Kirkby Stephen (07683) 71199
Appleby (07683) 51177
Carlisle (0228) 512444

Join the Friends of the Settle-Carlisle Line. Membership includes a quarterly newsletter which will keep you informed of news and events concerning the line.
Membership rates are:
Individual £4.00
Family £5.00
Corporate £10.00
Enclose SAE with your application, and make cheques/POs payable to FOSCL. Send to Ian Rodham, FOSCL Membership Secretary, 4, Lingwell Crescent, Leeds LS10 3SZ.

DalesRail excursions and guided walks from Leeds, Manchester and Preston are held on selected weekends. Leeds programme available

Castleberg Sports
OUTDOOR PURSUITS, SPORTS & LEISURE
HIRE OF BOOTS, BIKES, TENTS, ETC
CHILDRENS' BOOT EXCHANGE
Cheapside, Settle,
North Yorkshire
Tel: (0729) 823751

Before you go out there ...Take a look in here

L.D. MOUNTAIN CENTRE, is one of the country's leading specialist outdoor retailers.

Our Newcastle city centre shop has 5,000 sq feet of display area, stocked with comprehensive ranges from quality world famous brands, for example:

Clothing - **BERGHAUS, PATAGONIA, TENSON, SCHÖFFEL, THINK PINK, TROLL**

Rucsacs - **BERGHAUS, KARRIMOR**

Camping - **VANGO, PHOENIX**

Footwear - **SCARPA, LINE 7**

Climbing Hardware - **WILD COUNTRY, PETZL, EDELRID**

Serviced by our highly experienced and knowledgeable staff, our customer service is second to none.

Tel no. 091 221 0770. Fax no. 091 261 0922.

And don't forget if you can't call in, we have improved our International Mail Order Service – call our new number (091) 221 0770 or send us a fax on (091) 261 0922, we will be only too pleased to help.

LD mountain centre

Helping you enjoy the Great Outdoors

L.D. Mountain Centre, 34 Dean Street,
Newcastle upon Tyne NE1 1PG. Tel: (091) 232 3561

ATTENTION ALL WALKERS !

footprint produce complete full colour maps covering the routes of the Pennine Way (two maps), the Dalesway and the Cleveland Way. They include full descriptions of the route and list all essential information such as accommodation and transport.

"The complete map-guide"

Other titles available:-
West Highland Way, Ridegway
Our maps are available from your local book/outdoor shop or direct from:-
Footprint, Dept. LE, Unit 54,
STEP, Stirling FK7 7RP enclosing
£ 2.95 per map (inc. of p+p).

from Friends of DalesRail, 3 Rochester Terrace, Leeds LS6 3DF. Tel: (0532) 759645.

The Preston programme is available from Lancashire County Council, Surveyors and Bridgemasters Dept, PO Box 9, Guild House, Cross Street, Preston PR1 8RD. Tel: (0772) 263333.

There are regular steam-hauled train excursions along the Settle-Carlisle line. These special trains are not part of British Rail's schedule, but enthusiasts can find out what steam trains are running when and where, simply by calling Steamline, a telephone "hotline", on (0898) 881968.

Other Addresses

Yorkshire Dales National Park,
Colvend,
Hebden Road,
Grassington,
Skipton,
N Yorks BD23 5LB
Tel: (0756) 752748

Lake District National Park,
Busher Walk,
Kendal,
Cumbria LA9 4RH
Tel: (0539) 724555

North York Moors National Park,
The Old Vicarage,
Bondgate,

WALKING BOOTS, CLOTHING & EQUIPMENT

44 THE BANK, BARNARD CASTLE
CO. DURHAM DL12 8PN TEL: (0833) 37829

Outdoor World
Mountain Pursuits

RAMBLING - CLIMBING - BACKPACKING
LIGHTWEIGHT CAMPING - SKIING

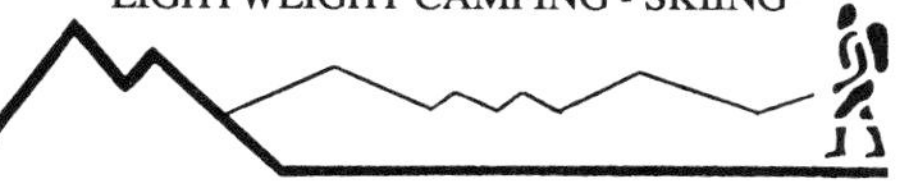

49 ILFRACOMBE GARDENS, WHITLEY BAY,
TYNE & WEAR, NE26 3LZ Tel: 091 251 4388

Bob Pocklington
Bedale Sports & Outdoors
Running Specialists
Well worth a visit
Good stocks, best brands, keen prices
Helpful friendly service
19 North End, Bedale, North Yorkshire
Phone & fax: (0677) 423746

Coast to Coast Walk
Special memorabilia

EMBROIDERED BADGES	£2.00
T-SHIRTS	£7.00
SWEAT SHIRTS	£11.00
ENAMEL LAPEL BADGES	£2.50
WALKING STICK MOUNTS	£3.00
MUGS	£2.00
COMPLETION CERTIFICATES	£0.50

North York Moors Adventure Centre

Park House
Ingleby Cross
Northallerton
North Yorkshire DL6 3PE
Tel: (060982) 571

Suppliers and distributors

Helmsley,
York YO6 5BP
Tel: (0439) 70657

Northumberland National Park,
Eastburn,
South Park,
Hexham,
Northumberland NE46 1BS
Tel: (0434) 605555

Peak National Park,
Aldern House,
Baslow Road,
Bakewell,
Derbyshire DE4 1AE

The Long Distance Walkers Association,
Membership Secretary,
7 Ford Drive,
Yarnfield,
Stone,
Staffs ST15 0RP
The aim of the association is "to further the interests of those who enjoy long-distance walking".

A magazine — called **Strider** — is published three times a year. Individual membership is currently £5.50. **The Long Distance Walkers' Handbook** (published by A & C Black) details some 280 walks in the UK.

The Ramblers' Association,
1-5 Wandsworth Road,
London SW8 2XX
Tel: (071) 582 6878
The association publishes **The Ramblers' Yearbook and Accommodation Guide**.

PRACTICAL COUNTRY CLOTHING

Inexpensive — hard wearing — top quality

For walking, fishing, shooting or working in the garden... the new Cudworth range has something for you. *Supercord* and *Supermole* trousers, waxed cotton, tweeds and cord jackets, shirts, skirts and blouses, bodywarmers, caps and much more.

- High quality, 95% British made
- Very competitive mail order prices
- Full money back guarantee
- Most orders despatched within 24 hours
- Over 100 years experience

Write for FREE brochure and price list to
Cudworth of Norden (Dept GNW)
Baitings Mill, Norden, Rochdale OL12 7TQ
Tel: (0706) 41771

By return dispatch of telephone orders (subject to stocks)

KENMAR CAMPING AND LEISURE

Spring Green Nurseries, Pontefract Road,
Sharlston, Wakefield, West Yorkshire
Tel: (0924) 864494
Large range of walking boots, outdoor clothing, backpacking equipment, family tents.
ALL AT COMPETITIVE PRICES

New ! ORDNANCE SURVEY MAPS

Laminated & Folded
Plastic Coated

Waterproof
Write-on surface

AVAILABLE FROM
YOUR USUAL SUPPLIER

Exclusively laminated and distributed by:
NORTHERN MAP DISTRIBUTORS
172 Psalter Lane
Sheffield S11 8UR
In case of difficulty, please phone (0742) 671128

Gordon Sargent

SPORTS EQUIPMENT
OUTDOOR GEAR

14 FINKLE STREET
RICHMOND
NORTH YORKSHIRE
DL10 4QB
Tel: Richmond (0748) 5376

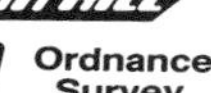

Barbour

SURVIVAL AIDS

Long Distance Paths Advisory Service,
Gerald Cole,
The Barn,
Holme Lyon,
Burneside,
Kendal,
Cumbria LA9 6QX
Tel: (0539) 727837

Countryside Commission,
John Dower House,
Crescent Place,
Cheltenham,
Glos GL50 3RA
Tel: (0242) 521381

Youth Hostels Association,
Trevelyan House,
8 St Stephen's Hill,
St Albans,
Herts AL1 2DY
Tel: (0727) 55215
The YHA have an annual publication: **YHA Accommodation Guide to England and Wales**. It lists all youth hostels, with maps, prices, opening hours, nearby attractions, and much more.

YHA Area Offices in the North:

Northern Region,
Bowey House,
William Street,
Newcastle-upon-Tyne,
Tyne & Wear NE3 1SA
Tel: (091) 221 2101

Lakeland,
Barclays Bank Chambers,
Crescent Road,
Windermere,
Cumbria LA23 1EA
Tel: (09662) 2301

Peak,
PO Box 11,
Matlock,
Derbyshire DE4 3XH
Tel: (0629) 584666

An excellent new idea comes from Footprint: long-distance walking maps which provide detailed route-finding and instructions, at a scale of approximately one inch to a mile.

The maps are in a linear format: that is, each strip of map covers the route itself and only a few miles either side. Distances are given at every mile, and the maps show other features such as phone boxes, mountain refuge huts and public transport access points.

Of the walks covered in this book the following Footprint maps are available: **The Pennine Way** (in two parts — Edale to Teesdale, and Teesdale to Kirk Yetholm) and the **Dales Way**. Other titles are in preparation.

Walking books from Leading Edge

The RailTrail Series

Pennine Rails and Trails — by John Morrison and Lydia Speakman, £5. 75

The Isle of Man by Tram, Train and Foot — by Stan Basnett and David Freke, £4.95

The Great Metro Guide to Tyne and Wear — by Vernon Abbott and Roy Chapman, £5.95

Exploring Strathclyde by Rail — by Tom Noble, £5.75

All available from your bookshop or direct from Leading Edge (Dept GNW), Old Chapel,Burtersett, Hawes, North Yorkshire DL8 3PB

Use our credit card ordering service, or write or phone for our up-to-date catalogue.

Postage & packing charges: 75p for single books; add £1 for orders over £10.

(0969) 667566